UNIT 1
THE OTHER SIDE OF THE

1   Australia quiz

True or false? Put a circle around the right letter.

		True	False
1	The south-west coast of Australia is crowded.	B	A
2	There are more Aborigines than people of European origin in Australia.	F	R
3	Uluru, the largest rock in the world, is well-known for its magical colours.	R	I
4	Christmas is in the Australian summer.	E	S
5	The first Europeans called the new continent 'down under'.	D	B
6	Today Australia is part of the British Empire.	A	N
7	Australians and Britons are rivals at cricket and rugby.	A	H
8	In the past most immigrants to Australia were British or Irish.	C	E

Read your letters from 8 to 1. You'll find the name of the Australian capital: _____ .

2   Australian cities

A geography teacher is telling his class how to complete the map of Australia. Listen and fill in the cities.

3   Aboriginal names

Look at the pictures and complete each definition.

1 A _____ is an Australian animal that moves by _____ on its back legs and that carries its young in a _____ of skin.

2 A _____ is an Aboriginal musical _____ that looks _____ a long wooden pipe* and makes a strange _____ .

3 A _____ is a curved* piece of _____ that returns when you _____ it in the right way. It was used by the _____ for hunting.

Canberra

*NEW: pipe – *Rohr*; curved – *gebogen*

Unit 1 **The other side of the world**

4   A crossword puzzle

Find the correct words or write the definitions.

1 to keep away from something or someone; to try not to do
2 _____
3 to say that you must do or have something
4 _____
   _____
5 _____
6 you notice it when you compare very different things
7 someone who travels to a place to find out about it
8 _____
9 _____
10 today
11 sleeping, not awake

→ The people who live down under: _____ .

Crossword answers shown: 2 HUGE, 4 BEAT, 5 ROCK, 8 ABORIGINES, 9 UPDATE

5   Small talk

Complete the conversations. Use the correct form of the verbs.

1 Adam   Hello, Alex. You (be) _____ a bit late, you know. I (wait) _____
          since half past seven.

   Alex   I'm sorry I'm late. I (just / write) _____ the last letter when Mr Miller
          (ask) _____ me to print out the new price lists. And, as usual, when I finally
          (arrive) _____ at the station, the train (just / leave) _____ .

   Adam   OK. I (already / buy) _____ the tickets for the film.

2 Kevin   Hello, Ryan. When (you / come) _____ back?

   Ryan   I (get) _____ back a minute ago actually.

   Kevin   (you / get) _____ the interview with Mrs Williams? You know the boss
          (wait) _____ for it.

   Ryan   No, I didn't. When I (arrive) _____ at her office, her secretary (tell)
          _____ me that Mrs Williams (already / leave) _____
          for Melbourne. Bad luck! She (not / return) _____ until Monday.

   Kevin   What a pity! The boss (not / be) _____ pleased about that.

3 Lara   I (see) _____ you yesterday outside the new burger place. Who (you / wait for)
          _____ ?

   Greg   Oh, I (show) _____ my cousin Andrew around. We (already / be) _____
          _____ on our feet for ages and we (be) _____ exhausted.
          We (want / have) _____ a snack before we (go) _____ to
          the cinema.

   Lara   Which film (you / see) _____ ?

   Greg   It (be) _____ called *Whale Rider*. It was really interesting.

6 Rabbit-Proof Fence

Fill in the gaps with suitable words or the correct form of the words in brackets.

Rabbit-Proof Fence is a film based on the real-life story of three Aborigine girls _____ walk hundreds of miles through the Australian outback to get home. Molly is 14 _____ old in 1931 when she, her eight-_____-old sister Daisy and their ten-year-old cousin Gracie (take) _____ from their home. Their mothers cry bitterly when the girls (force) _____ _____ to leave Jigalong in government cars. Jigalong, their small native village, is near the rabbit-proof fence, the (long) _____ fence in the world. The girls (send) _____ to Moore River Native Settlement near Perth. There they have to forget their _____ language and traditions and to learn to live _____ white people.

Most of the children at the camp don't have any memories of their mothers and families, but Molly knows that she has a mother and is determined to get _____ to her. When the girls see a chance, they _____ and disappear into the outback. All they have to do is find and follow the rabbit-proof fence, _____ goes right to Jigalong. Along the way there are many dangers: waterless deserts, hunger and the policemen _____ hunt the children. Molly, however, is a clever girl who manages _____ lead them home. The man who tries to make sure _____ the girls are returned to the camp is Chief Protector of the Aborigines, Mr Neville. The children call _____ 'Mr Devil'. He (genuine) _____ believes that he is doing the right thing. He (not / realize) _____ that separating children from their families is cruel. He (think) _____ the government's idea to make the children part of white society will help them to live better _____ .

Rabbit-Proof Fence is (certain) _____ one of the best films about this time – (Australia) _____ dark past from 1905 _____ 1971. The film is based on the book *Follow the Rabbit-Proof Fence* _____ Doris Pilkington, Molly's daughter.

7 New words

Use these verbs in their correct form to complete the sentences.

> apologize • damage • disappoint • reject • rise

1. A long time ago Bulari _____ from below the earth.
2. Aborigines try not to _____ the Earth.
3. In 1998 white society finally _____ to the Aborigines.
4. Cathy was happy that she had not _____ anyone.
5. She thinks that the Aborigines should not _____ their history and culture.

Unit 1 The other side of the world

8 True, false or not in the text?

Put a circle around the right letter.   True   False   NIT

1. When Bulari first came to Australia, there weren't any mountains or valleys.   E   R   A
2. The rainbow snake made the plants and the animals.   D   M   R
3. The Aborigines didn't kill animals.   B   I   T
4. The Aborigines regarded the white settlers as primitive people.   O   S   T
5. Cathy Freeman was a member of the 'stolen generation'.   N   M   P
6. The Aborigines weren't given equal rights until 1967.   A   D   E
7. In 1998 thousands of Aborigines rejected National Sorry Day.   F   H   E
8. The Union Jack is part of the Australian flag.   I   K   R
9. When Cathy Freeman carried two flags, she had a message for Aborigines.   D   E   L

Read your letters from 9 to 1. You'll find the Aboriginal name for the beginning of the world: _____ .

9 Which word is it?

Read the definitions and find the right words. They are all in Text 1.

1. It's an arch of beautiful colours that appears in the sky when the sun shines through rain. _____
2. all the things in the world that were not made by people, such as plants, animals and rivers: _____
3. the ideas, language or art of a group of people: _____
4. It's an illness* like a bad cold. You usually have a temperature and a headache. _____
5. to be the most successful in a competition, race, etc.: _____
6. to say you are sorry for something you have said or done: _____

*NEW: illness – *Krankheit*

10 Say it in German

Lies die Zeilen 47–57 von Text 1 und vervollständige diesen deutschen Text.

Die junge Cathy war eine _____ und sie hatte einen Traum. Im jugendlichen Alter _____ _____ .

Sie trainierte _____ .

Zu ihrem Training gehörten _____ _____ – ihre Familie _____ _____ , neue Laufschuhe zu kaufen. In den neunziger Jahren _____ _____ . Sie war jung und schön, voller Mut und _____ . 1997 wurde sie _____ und wurde zur ‚Australierin des Jahres' ernannt.

The other side of the world Unit 1

11 Missing words

Find the missing words. They are all in Text 1.

1 apprenticeship → apprentice ● immigration → _immigrant_
2 defensive → defense ● ambitious → _____
3 surfing → surfboard ● running → _____
4 go on → give up ● find → _____
5 stream → river ● pool → _____
6 rose → flower ● swallow → _____
7 say again → repeat ● not do → _____
8 happy → unhappy ● fortunate → _____
9 poison → poisonous ● poverty → _____
10 competition → compete ● decision* → _____

*NEW: decision – Entscheidung

12 Say it in words you know!

1 What do the words in brackets mean? Say it in words you already know.

1 When you wear (*Flossen*) _____
_____, you can swim faster.

2 Let's sit under (*dem Sonnenschirm*) _____
_____. I can't stay in the sun any longer.

3 My friend suffered from (*Müdigkeit durch die Zeitverschiebung*) _____
_____.

4 The Sydney Opera House is a famous (*Wahrzeichen*) _____
_____.

5 Is the koala bear (*ein Beuteltier*) _____
_____ like the kangaroo?

6 Are there any (*Rettungsschwimmer*) _____
_____ on Bondi Beach?

2 Now fill in the right sentence number for the words below:

the sunshade ☐   lifeguards ☐   a marsupial ☐
jet lag ☐   landmark ☐   flippers ☐

13 A text message quiz

Read these words like text messages. Be careful, each number can stand for different letters. For example 4 stands for G, H and I. Find six words from Unit 1.

1 28255263 _____
2 439737 _____
3 286433 _____
4 759348464 _____
5 6882225 _____
6 6883667 _____

five 5

Unit 1 The other side of the world

14 Going to New Zealand

Complete the conversations. Use *going to* (a plan), *will* (a sudden idea), the present progressive (a fixed plan) and the simple present (a timetable).

Yesterday Michael went to a travel agency to buy a ticket to Auckland. He also reserved a hotel room. On his way home he met his friend Sally.

Michael   I (fly) _____ to New Zealand next January.

Sally   Wow! I've got nothing special on in January. I think I (come) _____ with you.

Michael   Great! Let's go to the travel agency together. We (get) _____ another ticket for you straight away.

Ten minutes later they were back at the travel agency.

Travel agent   Your plane (leave) _____ at 7:35 on January 9th. Here is your programme. You (stay) _____ on the North Island from January 12th to 17th.

Sally   (we / visit) _____ Rotorua as well?

Michael   Of course. I can't wait! Do you know where I can buy a book about New Zealand?

Travel agent   Well, there's a bookshop in Merton Street. They have lots of guidebooks.

Sally   You go to the bookshop, and I think I (buy) _____ some clothes for our trip.

Travel agent   You'd better be quick. The shops (close) _____ in 20 minutes.

15 Snorkelling and diving

Fill in the missing passive and active verb forms.

New Zealand (see) _____ by many as the home of adventure sports. It's the ideal place for all outdoor activities, and the same is true of neighbouring Australia. Snorkelling* and diving* in this part of the world (can / only / describe) _____ as spectacular. So why (you / not / go) _____ to one of Australia's greatest attractions, the Great Barrier Reef? It (stretch*) _____ for more than 1,600 miles off the coast of Queensland and (must / certain / call) _____ one of the world's natural wonders. Its tiny corals* (join) _____ together and form colonies. The Great Barrier Reef (begin / grow) _____ very slowly two million years ago, and today it (be) _____ one of the largest living attractions in the world.

Thousands of ships (destroy) _____ at the Great Barrier Reef over the centuries. It (hit) _____ by Captain Cook's *Endeavour*, too. Just imagine, if this ship (sink) _____ , Australia's history (be) _____ very different! If you (go) _____ diving with an instructor, you (take) _____ to a magical world of colour. But be careful if you (meet) _____ by a nice little golf-ball-sized octopus*: it (bite) _____ and kill you within minutes.

*NEW: snorkelling – *Schnorcheln*; diving – *Tauchen*; to stretch – *sich erstrecken*; coral – *Koralle*; octopus – *Tintenfisch*

The other side of the world **Unit 1**

16 The Kiwi Experience

3 1 Listen to the first part of Text 2. Six words in this text are wrong. Underline them and write the correct words above the wrong ones.

> Two friends, Jane and Deirdre, took a year off from their jobs in England and travelled round the world. During their trip, they spent a month in New Zealand. In the South Ireland they visited Queenstown, the exciting capital of the country, on the banks of the beautiful Lake Wakatipu. Lots of young pupils go there to do bungee jumping, skydiving and other kinds of extra activities. There are several places where you can do a bungee jump, including the Kawarau Building, the world's first commercial jump site.

4 2 Listen to the second part of Text 2 and answer these questions about a special day in Jane's diary. You don't have to write complete sentences.

1	On which day of the week did they jump?	
2	Why were they weighed?	
3	Why didn't they want to dip their heads into the water?	
4	How did Jane feel up there?	
5	Where did they jump from?	
6	How often did Jane bounce up and down?	
7	How did she get back to the river bank?	

5 3 Listen to the last part of Text 2 and tick (✓) the correct ending.

1 The Maoris say that the Franz Josef glacier was made from the tears of …
   A ☐ a lovesick boy.   B ☐ a lonely mother.   C ☐ a lovesick girl.
2 Before Jane and Deirdre could climb the glacier, they had to …
   A ☐ borrow equipment.   B ☐ learn to climb.   C ☐ wait for a helicopter.
3 The top of the glacier was hidden by …
   A ☐ ants.   B ☐ the clouds.   C ☐ people.
4 The group had to stop every 20 minutes because …
   A ☐ it was so cold.   B ☐ it was so beautiful.   C ☐ it was hard work and they were tired.

17 The bungee jump

Your dream has come true: you have done your first bungee jump! Your teacher has asked you to e-mail the class a short report about this adventure. Answer the following questions in your e-mail and add two aspects of your own. Write about 140 words in your exercise book.

- Where/When did it happen?
- Why did you decide to do it?
- Who went with you?
- What did you think before the jump?
- How did you feel afterwards?

seven **7**

Unit 1 The other side of the world

18 Paraphrasing

Paraphrase the words in bold. Do not change the meaning of the sentences.

1 Two friends, Jane and Deirdre, **took** a year **off from their jobs** and travelled round the world.
   Two friends, Jane and Deirdre, _____ and travelled round the world.

2 This morning **a minibus took us** from our hostel to the site.
   This morning _____ to get from our hostel to the site.

3 We decided we **would stay dry**.
   We decided we _____ .

4 … and then **it was my turn**.
   … and then _____ .

5 … **we were surrounded by** ice and snow.
   … _____ ice and snow _____ .

19 The kiwi

Fill in the missing prepositions.

Look _____ this small fat bird! It is nocturnal*, which means that it comes _____ when the sun goes _____ . The kiwi can't fly because _____ its weight so it lives _____ the ground. Its feathers* are different _____ those of other birds – they look like brown hair. Its eggs are huge compared _____ the size of the adult bird, but the little ones are independent _____ the start. They like to eat anything they can catch: they look _____ berries and other fruit, but they prefer spiders and worms*. _____ the way, kiwis can choose _____ 192 different kinds _____ worms _____ New Zealand. The Maoris named the bird _____ the sound _____ its call: 'creee, creee'. There's no other country where it could survive because everywhere else the kiwi would have too many enemies.

The kiwi fruit came _____ China _____ New Zealand _____ a hundred years ago. It tastes like a mixture _____ strawberries and other fruit. This green fruit, _____ its brown skin covered _____ short hair, is exported _____ lots _____ other countries. It was named _____ the bird. Most _____ the world's kiwi come _____ New Zealand (June _____ October) and California (November _____ May).
Today the kiwi bird and the kiwi fruit have become national symbols _____ New Zealand and the word 'kiwi' is also used informally _____ the New Zealand dollar and _____ the people who live there!

*NEW: nocturnal – *nachtaktiv*; feather – *Feder*; worm – *Wurm*

20 Grandmother

Lies den Text und beantworte die folgenden Fragen stichpunktartig auf Deutsch.

1 *Wieso wurde der Erzähler von seiner Großmutter abgeholt?*

2 *Mit welcher Sprache ist der Erzähler aufgewachsen und welche andere Sprache beherrscht er?*

3 *Warum imitierten die Maori die Sitten und Bräuche der Europäer?*

4 *Beschreibe das äußere Erscheinungsbild der Großmutter (drei unterschiedliche Details):*

5 *Welche zwei gegensätzlichen Charakterzüge zeigten sich im Verhältnis der Großmutter zu ihrem Enkel?*

6 *Wozu forderte die Großmutter ihren Enkel auf, als sie bemerkte, dass er erwachsen wurde? (drei Details)*

10 points   Key p. 43

21 The Crocodile Hunter

You are going to hear an Australian news report. While listening: take notes on an extra sheet so that you can answer the questions. After listening: write the answers in your workbook. You don't have to write complete sentences, but one word is not enough.

1 Where could the news report be heard?
   Radio Station: _____

2 What happened to Steve Irwin? _____

3 What was Irwin doing when he was killed? _____

4 What was Irwin known for? (two details)

5 What do we learn about Irwin's family? (two details)

6 How did the Australian Prime Minister describe Steve Irwin? (three details)

10 points   Key p. 43   *NEW: stingray – *Stachelrochen*

CHECK OUT A

1 Who or what is it?

1 The _____ is the winner in a sports competition.
2 Something is _____ when it frightens you.
3 A _____ is a worker on a farm.
4 A _____ is a field of ice on a mountain.
5 A _____ is a piece of paper which shows the amount of money you have paid.
6 The _____ is the area of Australia that is a long way from the coast and towns.
7 A _____ is what people wear when they go swimming.
8 You need a _____ in order to change a wheel.
9 The _____ are the people who settled in Australia first.
10 In the _____ you can see huge plants and wild animals.

2 Complete the text about an Australian lifesaver from Bondi Beach using suitable tenses.

Jim Marsh (work) _____ ¹ as a lifesaver for 31 years now. He (stop) _____ ² working next month. I (know) _____ ³ him since he moved in next door. I (be) _____ ⁴ six years old then and he (teach) _____ ⁵ me how to swim. Although he's now 52, he (surf) _____ ⁶ every day. Last week when I arrived at Bondi Beach, he (carry) _____ ⁷ his surfboard into the water. 'Hi, Jim,' I shouted when we were getting out of the water, 'would you like to come to our barbecue?' – 'I think I (have) _____ ⁸ plenty of time for barbecues from next month,' he answered. But after he (put) _____ ⁹ his board away, we went to our house and an evening of steak and sausages (enjoy) _____ ¹⁰ by all.

3 Guided writing

You went on a trip round New Zealand and Australia with Kiwi and Koala Tours. Some of the information advertised on the internet turned out to be wrong. Write a letter of complaint in your exercise book (about 140 words) and mention the following aspects:

accommodation

guidebooks

entrance fees

KIWI AND KOALA TOURS
See New Zealand and Australia in 24 days
The price includes:
- comfortable rooms in first-class hotels
- all transport in air-conditioned buses
- free guidebooks for New Zealand and Australia
- all entrance fees
- trip to Milford Sound
- a meal while watching the sun set near Ayers Rock

FROM $4,599

trip to Milford Sound

an additional aspect

Key p. 43 | 20 points

UNIT 2
FACT OR FICTION?

1 FAQs

1 Match the right parts. Will we be able to:

1 develop   A other solar systems?
2 choose   B asteroids for metal?
3 set up   C animals and humans?
4 mine   D a personality?
5 explore   E new drugs to fight disease?
6 clone   F colonies on other planets?

1	
2	
3	
4	
5	
6	

  2 You will hear five people answering some questions. Listen to their answers (A–E) and decide what topic (1–5) the people are talking about.

1 greenhouse gases
2 sea levels
3 genetic engineering
4 space travel
5 human clones

1	
2	
3	
4	
5	

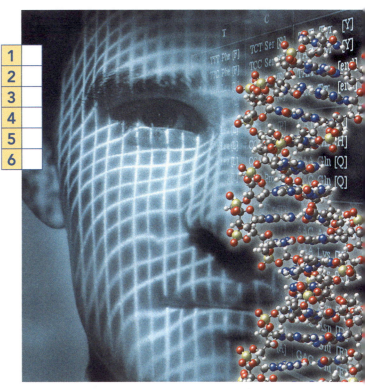

2 Genetic engineering

Complete the German translations.

1 Genes are the parts of cells that determine what a living thing will be like.

   Gene sind Bestandteile von Zellen, _____
   _____ .

2 Using genetic engineering, scientists can take genes from one living thing and put them into another one. _____ , können Wissenschaftler einem Lebewesen Gene entnehmen und in ein anderes einsetzen.

3 After finding a special gene, scientists can cut it out and transplant it.

   _____ ,
   können Wissenschaftler es herausschneiden und transplantieren.

4 After receiving the gene of an Arctic fish, a tomato plant can resist the cold.

   _____ ,
   kann eine Tomatenpflanze kältebeständig sein.

5 Believing that genetic engineering can create better crops, scientists go on with their research.

   _____ ,
   setzen Wissenschaftler ihre Forschung fort.

6 By developing rice that has more vitamin A, they hope to help millions of kids.
   _____ , hoffen sie,
   Millionen von Kindern helfen zu können.

7 Many people fear that plants carrying new genes could be dangerous for the environment or humans.

   Viele Leute fürchten, _____ ,
   gefährlich für die Umwelt oder Menschen sein könnten.

Unit 2 Fact or fiction?

3 Internet attacks

Tick (✓) the correct long forms of the phrases in green. Sometimes more than one form is correct.

1 In February 2006 a fast-moving internet worm **attacking hundreds of thousands of computers worldwide** hit the headlines and started yet another scare.

   A ☐ which was attacked by hundreds of thousands of computers worldwide
   B ☐ whose hundreds of thousands of computers were attacked worldwide
   C ☐ which attacked hundreds of thousands of computers worldwide

2 The worm was called Nyxem and destroyed files on computers **using certain versions of Microsoft software** on the 3rd day of every month.

   A ☐ that wanted to use certain versions of Microsoft software
   B ☐ which were used by certain versions of Microsoft software
   C ☐ which used certain versions of Microsoft software

3 **Knowing about the security* hole** in their software, Microsoft had advised users to download a special update to protect their computers.

   A ☐ As they knew about the security hole
   B ☐ Because they knew about the security hole
   C ☐ Although they knew about the security hole

4 Some time before, FBI agents arrested an 18-year-old student from Minnesota **after searching the student's home**. He had created a different computer worm.

   A ☐ after the student had searched his home
   B ☐ after they had searched the student's home
   C ☐ after they had searched for the student's home

5 **Admitting that he had created the Blaster B internet worm**, the student was sent to prison.

   A ☐ Because he admitted that he had created the Blaster B internet worm
   B ☐ Before he admitted that he had created the Blaster B internet worm
   C ☐ While he admitted that he had created the Blaster B internet worm

6 Why do people create computer worms or viruses? It's the same psychology **driving people to set fire to things or spray graffiti on walls**.

   A ☐ which drives people to set fire to things or spray graffiti on walls
   B ☐ who people drive to set fire to things or spray graffiti on walls
   C ☐ whose people are driven to set fire to things or spray graffiti on walls

7 Hackers want to show that they are more intelligent than the companies **making the programs**.

   A ☐ whose programs are made
   B ☐ which make the programs
   C ☐ that make the programs

8 Maybe they don't realize that they cause* real problems for computer users. Even a silly message can lead to difficulties, **forcing users to waste time**.

   A ☐ while users force them to waste time
   B ☐ because users are forced to waste time
   C ☐ as users force them to waste time

*NEW: security – *Sicherheit*; to cause – *verursachen*

4 Dolly the copy sheep

Choose the correct participle to complete each sentence. Put a line through the wrong form.

1 Dolly was the first animal cloned / cloning by scientists in 1996. Dolly was the exact genetic copy of another sheep.
2 The man led / leading the experiment was Dr Ian Wilmut of the Roslin Institute near Edinburgh, Scotland.
3 A cell taken / taking from an adult sheep was treated so that the egg cell of another sheep accepted its DNA.
4 Implanted* / Implanting into that sheep, the egg cell developed into the sheep called / calling Dolly, the first clone.
5 Scientists worked / working on cloning projects say that cloning isn't easy or cheap. It took them 277 tries to produce Dolly, but unfortunately she died quite young at the age of six.
6 There are growing numbers of animal clones – pigs, cats, mice and cattle. Frightened / Frightening by this development, lots of people wonder if the world will soon see a human clone.

5 A crossword puzzle

Fill in the missing words.

1 a scientific test
2 someone who writes computer software
3 except if
4 to beat, win against
5 something that might happen or become true
6 unable to breathe because you can't get enough air
7 to plan
8 to say that something will happen

6 Global warming

Tick (✓) the correct German translation.

1 A report written by international scientists in 2002 said that the 1990s were the warmest ten years for centuries.
→ Ein Bericht,   A ☐ der im Jahr 2002 für internationale Wissenschaftler geschrieben wurde,
   B ☐ der im Jahr 2002 von internationalen Wissenschaftlern geschrieben wurde,
besagte, dass die 1990er-Jahre die wärmsten zehn Jahre seit Jahrhunderten waren.

2 Most people agree that carbon dioxide produced when we burn gas or oil is the biggest environmental problem.
→ Die meisten Leute stimmen zu, dass Kohlendioxid,
   A ☐ das erzeugt wird, wenn wir Gas oder Öl verbrennen, das größte Umweltproblem ist.
   B ☐ wenn wir Gas oder Öl verbrennen, das größte Umweltproblem erzeugt.

3 Paid by international oil companies, some scientists say that global warming doesn't exist.
→ A ☐ Nachdem sie für internationale Ölgesellschaften bezahlten,
   B ☐ Da/Weil sie von internationalen Ölgesellschaften bezahlt werden,
sagen einige Wissenschaftler, dass die globale Erwärmung nicht existiert.

4 Others say that there are more and more disasters caused by global warming.
→ Andere sagen, dass es immer mehr Katastrophen gibt,
   A ☐ die eine globale Erwärmung verursachen.
   B ☐ die durch die globale Erwärmung verursacht werden.

*NEW: to implant – *implantieren, einpflanzen*

Unit 2 Fact or fiction?

7 Six verbs

> beep • exploit • gain • interrupt • involve • prevent

Find the right verb for each gap and use it in its correct form.

1 Many children in developing countries often have to work hard and are _____ .
2 When the camera starts _____ , you should replace the battery.
3 You will have to _____ some experience before you can apply for that kind of job.
4 Four cars and one lorry were _____ in the accident.
5 The exams don't _____ her from going to discos.
6 Please stop _____ me when I'm talking.

8 Whiz-Kids

1 Listen to the first part of Text 1. Six words in this text are wrong. Underline them and write the correct words above the wrong ones.

Samuel Albright is sitting in his home office staring at the computer screen. The young webmaster works for an e-mail company called Nets@les. He is exhausted, but he is trying to concentrate on a new design program. The program will help him to create the online firms used by customers. Samuel has to finish the job by Friday. It is sometimes difficult for him to get through the requested amount of work. But his spare-time job is exciting and undoubtedly trendy. He earns 25,000 dollars a month, but if you watch him, you'll recognize that he's been bitten by the bug, and he doesn't just do it for the money.

2 Listen to the second part of Text 1 and tick (✓) the correct answer.

1 Samuel knows that …
 A ☐ his job is more important than school.
 B ☐ school must come first.
 C ☐ Nets@les won't give him another job.

2 Samuel doesn't …
 A ☐ think about his future.
 B ☐ work part-time for Nets@les now.
 C ☐ deny that he wants to be successful.

3 Listen to the last part of Text 1. While listening: take notes on an extra sheet so that you can answer the questions. After listening: write the answers in your workbook. You don't have to write complete sentences, but one word is not enough.

1 Which companies do whiz-kids usually work for? (two)
  _____
2 Where did Samuel get his computer knowledge from?
  _____
3 Why doesn't Samuel play computer games?
  _____
4 What can Kim's friends do while she's in front of her computer?
  _____
5 How was her cousin John exploited by a company?
  _____
6 Where will Samuel and Kim probably work in the future? _____

14 fourteen

9 Words

Find the missing words.

1. compete → competitor ● design → _____
2. invent → invention ● know → _____
3. war → peace ● disease → _____
4. village → town ● part-time → _____
5. give back → return ● a rest → _____
6. invader → invade ● employer → _____
7. beautiful → lovely ● (school) mark → _____
8. exciting → excitement ● interesting → _____
9. scared → frightened ● mistake → _____
10. communicate → communication ● succeed → _____

10 A crossword puzzle

Find the correct words.

1. [ˈdedlaɪn]
2. [ˈwebmɑːstə]
3. [ɪnˈʃʊərəns]
4. [wɪz]
5. [ˈtʃælɪndʒ]
6. [dɪˈmɑːndɪŋ]

→ Jade is studying graphic _____ .

11 Riddle-me-ree

This is a riddle-me-ree puzzle. You can find out the name of a device for your camera.

1. My first is in **FORM** and also in **ITEM**.
2. My second is in **STAGE** but not in **GAS**.
3. My third is in **WARM** and also in **MOOD**.
4. My fourth is in **LION** and also in **BOX**.
5. My fifth is in **RASTA** but not in **LAST**.
6. My sixth is in **MAY** and also in **YES**.
7. My seventh is in **COAL** but not in **LOAD**.
8. My eighth is in **ABBEY** and also in **GAIN**.
9. My ninth is in **BRAIN** but not in **BANKING**.
10. My tenth is in **DEADLINE** and also in **STUDY**.

Riddle me, riddle me, riddle-me-ree! Which device is it?

_____

12 Busy whiz-kids

Link these sentences. Use each of the words in the box at least once.

> although • as soon as • because • if • since • so that • until

1. My mother is angry. I have been sitting at my computer for hours again.
   _____
2. I might join our school's basketball team. My mom will be very happy.
   _____
3. I'm not very good at volleyball. I am interested in it, however.
   _____
4. Whiz-kids have to get a proper education. Then they can get to the top.
   _____
5. Samuel gets up. Next, he switches on his computer.
   _____
6. Samuel started to work on a new website three days ago. He hasn't met his friends since then.
   _____
7. He couldn't stop working on an interesting project. But then his friends complained.
   _____
8. Samuel phoned his colleague Kim. He thought she should know about the new deadline.
   _____

Unit 2 Fact or fiction?

13 The big blackout
Find words to complete the text.

On August 14, 2003, the largest blackout* in American history left 50 million people _____ light, air conditioning or electricity. Power went out at 4:11 P.M. in eight states and dozens of cities in the north-_____ of the US and in Canada, including New York, Detroit, Cleveland and Toronto. When the computer _____ went dark and the telephones stopped _____ , thousands of people rushed out* of their buildings into the streets. No subway trains were running, buses were extremely full, and traffic soon came to a standstill. Lots of people were stuck in the subway system or in elevators, _____ for rescue workers to reach them. People tried to _____ their families or friends, but even cellphones failed to work. Hundreds of people weren't _____ to get home and had to spend the _____ sleeping on the sidewalks.
What had happened? Experts couldn't immediately say _____ had led to the power cut. At least they were quickly able to say that the blackout was not a terrorist _____ .
People in New York noticed strange activities – ice-cream sellers tried to sell at _____ prices. Their prices dropped from $3 to $1, but hot dog prices went _____ amazingly. A young man _____ around shouting 'flashlights* $25, batteries $10'.
On Times Square, _____ tourists usually photograph the _____ , the darkness was the main attraction of the evening. As there weren't enough police officers, ordinary people acted as traffic police standing in the middle of intersections, stopping and starting the _____ . The people of Manhattan stood in the streets, talking and laughing with each _____ .
Others played musical _____ for them. The most important _____ was that the city had stayed calm. There was no looting* and little violence. After more _____ 24 hours, the whole area was almost back to normal again. The _____ blackout in the nation's history is said to _____ about six billion dollars.

16 sixteen

*NEW: blackout – *Stromausfall*; to rush out – *hinauseilen*; flashlight – *Taschenlampe*; looting – *Plünderei*

Fact or fiction? Unit 2

14 Indian whiz-kids in Germany

Fill in the correct form of the verbs in brackets.

If you (be interested / see) _____ a modern opera about an Indian computer expert, you (must / come) _____ and see *IndierInnen*. It's the story of Soraya, an intelligent Indian woman, and what happened to her when she was forced to go to Germany to earn money working for a computer company.

If her disabled husband, Mahatma, hadn't borrowed so much money to pay for her education, she (never / think) _____ about going abroad. And if she hadn't agreed to work in Europe, she (not / be able / pay) _____ for her husband's operation. Soon feeling exploited by her employers, Soraya organized a protest by Indian workers. If she (not / do) _____ that, she (not / go) _____ _____ to prison and (not / need) _____ her husband's help once again. He had been operated on by that time and saved her from the computer industry. But then, strangely, he told her, 'I can work again. If I (earn) _____ the money, you (can / stay) _____ at home and do the housework.'

People wouldn't enjoy this strange story so much if it (not / show) _____ true facts about the lives of workers in the modern computer industry.

15 Schools with a difference

Find the synonyms (>>) and opposites (><) of the words in brackets.

There are (>< exactly) _____ 220,000 children in the US who would love to be (>< learned) _____ at a state school, but they don't have the possibility. Their families are homeless. The parents (>< find) _____ their jobs more (>< slowly) _____ than others and then they (>> start) _____ a new life somewhere else. But now there is a 50-year-old (>< pupil) _____ in a caravan who (>> cares for) _____ these (>> kids) _____ : Agnes Stevens from Los Angeles. She's one of (>< less) _____ than 400 volunteers* who make it seem like Christmas when they (>< take) _____ a child a backpack full of school materials and books. When the kids move away again, they can (>> phone) _____ an 800 number so that School on Wheels can (>< receive) _____ a tutor to their new home – a car, a motel or out on the street. Much (>< nearer) _____ south, in the Amazon rainforest, there's another (>> huge) _____ team of volunteers working in schools which are also very (>< same) _____ from the normal American state school. In some areas, children have to go to school by boat, and when they (>> get there) _____ , there's only one classroom. But as one volunteer says, 'You can't leave these small faces with their bright eyes (>> except if) _____ your heart is made of stone.'

*NEW: volunteer – *Freiwillige/r*

Unit 2 Fact or fiction?

16 Dictionary work

The following words have various meanings. Which of the meanings given in the dictionary is the one used in Text 2? Underline the best German translation.

notice (line 10)
(VERB) **1 beachten, Notiz nehmen von**
2 bemerken *Did you notice her dress? Hast du ihr Kleid bemerkt?*
(NOMEN) **3 Kündigung** She handed in her notice last Friday. *Sie reichte letzten Freitag ihre Kündigung ein.*
4 Bescheid 5 Schild

past (line 41)
(NOMEN) **1** *Grammatik* **Vergangenheitsform**
2 Vergangenheit
(ADJ) **3 vergangen** in the past few months *in den letzten Monaten*
(PRÄP) **4 nach** It's ten past five. *Es ist zehn nach fünf.*
5 an … vorbei He walked straight past her. *Er ging einfach an ihr vorbei.* **6 über … hinaus**

cover (box)
(VERB) **1 mit Decke, Deckel usw. bedecken, zudecken**
2 *Dach* **decken**
3 *Oberfläche* **bedecken** The floor was covered with flowers. *Der Fußboden war mit Blumen bedeckt.*
4 *Fläche* **sich erstrecken über**
5 *Presse* **berichten über**

fit (box)
(ADJ) **1 fit, gesund** She keeps fit by swimming. *Sie hält sich durch Schwimmen fit.*
2 geeignet
(NOMEN) **3 Anfall** a fit of coughing *ein Hustenanfall*
(VERB) **4 hineinpassen in**
5 *Kleidung* **passen**

17 The Eden Project

Tick (✓) the correct information about Text 2. Sometimes more than one ending is correct.

1 Hannah and Ellie …
 A ☐ know every plant in the rainforest.
 B ☐ don't like lizards.
 C ☐ are looking for Alex and Josh.
2 The waterfall …
 A ☐ was a quiet place.
 B ☐ sprayed the visitors.
 C ☐ came down the roof of the greenhouse.
3 The name cola …
 A ☐ comes from a tropical bush.
 B ☐ is Roman in origin.
 C ☐ comes from East Africa.
4 A bamboo house …
 A ☐ can have more than one storey.
 B ☐ is stronger than an earthquake.
 C ☐ is very cheap.
5 Hannah doesn't want …
 A ☐ to return to the top.
 B ☐ to stay in the humid air any longer.
 C ☐ to wait outside.

18 Who thought this?

Fill in the names.

1 'I hope I can get out of here quite soon.' _____
2 'Where are the girls?' _____
3 'Oh, I think I'll drink some now.' _____
4 'And what if we meet a tiger in here???' _____
5 'I'd like to live in one of these.' _____
6 'Why don't we go to the top next?' _____

19 Frogs Are Friends

You have to present a short paper in biology. Your parents tell you about the organization Frogs Are Friends. They help frogs near busy streets on rainy nights. The helpers carry the frogs across before there is a deadly accident. You think that's rather strange, but it's the perfect topic for your paper. Write a letter of about 140 words to get some information about this organization. Think about these points and use your exercise book.

☞ how many people work for them
☞ who had the idea
☞ how many hours a year they spend saving frogs
☞ results
☞ brochures/websites
☞ and add two aspects of your own

Start like this:

Dear Sir or Madam, / Dear Frogs Are Friends,
I have heard about …

Fact or fiction? Unit 2

20 The Hitchhiker's Guide to the Galaxy

Read the text and decide whether the following statements are true, false or not in the text.

		True	False	Not in the text
1	The three extracts are about Arthur Dent and his friend Douglas Adams who escape from Earth before it is destroyed.	☐	☐	☐
2	The two friends always meet on Thursdays.	☐	☐	☐
3	The Vogons want to demolish the Earth because it's standing in the way of an expressway.	☐	☐	☐
4	The Vogons can understand the feelings of the people on Earth.	☐	☐	☐
5	Arthur tells Ford not to panic after the demolition.	☐	☐	☐
6	The fish in your ear helps you hear things more clearly.	☐	☐	☐

21 Finish the sentences

Use the information from the text to complete the sentences.

1 The two friends have known each other _____.

2 The Vogons used a public address system _____
_____.

3 Everybody on Earth should have known about the demolition because _____
_____.

4 Ford was able to rescue Arthur by _____.

| 10 points | Key p. 44 |

22 Environmental issues in the news

Part 1: You will hear four news reports about pollution* and other problems in the world. What are the reports (A–D) about? Listen and write the correct letter in the box.

1 computer waste ☐   4 water pollution ☐
2 noise pollution ☐   5 floods ☐
3 air pollution ☐   6 rainforests ☐

*NEW: pollution – *Umweltverschmutzung*

Part 2: Listen to the next report. Tick (✓) the correct endings to the following sentences. Be careful, sometimes more than one ending is correct.

7 The new robot called Spyke …
   A ☐ is the perfect Christmas present for parents and children.
   B ☐ can't be bought for under £200.
   C ☐ must have presents for Christmas.

8 It can help you if …
   A ☐ you need things to be done around the house.
   B ☐ you can't do your homework.
   C ☐ you keep forgetting to turn the lights off.

9 Spyke can be used as …
   A ☐ a telephone.
   B ☐ an MP3 player.
   C ☐ a power station.

10 The robot industry …
   A ☐ is led by Microsoft.
   B ☐ is now in the same situation as computers in the mid-1970s.
   C ☐ is owned by a Japanese company.

| 10 points | Key p. 44 |

CHECK YOUR READING

CHECK YOUR LISTENING

CHECK OUT B

1 Find the correct nouns.

Lots of people don't see the _____¹ for projects which are as expensive as the Eden Project in Cornwall. But _____² say that this experiment is of great _____³ because of all the _____⁴ we have gained. It has been a _____⁵ while other attempts* to find a _____⁶ to problems by _____⁷ and error have failed. There is also a chance of earning a lot of money in the tourist _____⁸ and there aren't any _____⁹ with similar _____¹⁰ in the area.

*NEW: attempt – Versuch

> necessary
> scientific
> important
> know • successful
> solve
> try
> busy
> compete • attractive

2 Complete the text about an Italian thief using suitable verb forms.

An Italian thief has been caught after failing to steal a digital camera. If Lucia Balta (not / look) _____¹ into her neighbour's flat, she (not / see) _____² the nice jewellery and the digital camera lying on the table. She thought, 'If I (take) _____³ the things and put them in my rucksack, no one (notice) _____⁴.' But then she decided to put the camera back on the table because she thought it was old and not worth stealing.
A police spokesman said, 'If you (put) _____⁵ a camera down too hard, it (take) _____⁶ a picture. We tried it several times and it worked every time. If the thief (realize) _____⁷ the camera had taken her picture, she (not / leave) _____⁸ it behind, I think.'
The police identified her after the owner of the flat came back to find the jewellery missing and an extra picture on his digital camera. After being arrested, the thief told the police, 'If I (be) _____⁹ as rich as my neighbour, I (not / steal) _____¹⁰ his things.'

3 Guided writing

You have just bought a new computer. Write an e-mail of about 140 words to your Australian penfriend about the computer and mention the following aspects:

- when and where you got it;
- why you wanted a new computer;
- what's special about it;
- what you normally use it for;
- ???
- ???

(Find two more aspects of your own!)

UNIT 3
FOREVER YOUNG

1 A crossword

1. the time of your life when you are young
2. to join or mix things together
3. a person whose job it is to play or write music
4. a day or period when people celebrate something
5. the style of clothes that is popular at a time
   → It started in the 1950s in the US: _____.
6. a period of ten years
7. an effect on somebody or something
8. becoming wider towards the bottom
9. part of a town where people of the same race or religion live, often in poor conditions
10. a type of slow, sad music
11. to become widely known
12. an old story or a famous person or event

2 The history of jeans

Each verb in brackets should be a *to*-infinitive or an *ing*-form. Be careful, sometimes you have to add a preposition.

In 1848 gold was found in California and thousands of people started (look) _____ for it. As they had (work) _____ hard, they wanted strong trousers. A clever businessman from Bavaria managed (produce) _____ the right type of trousers: blue jeans. Soon farmers and cowboys as well as people working in mines enjoyed (wear) _____ them. In the 1930s Hollywood began (make) _____ western movies. Cowboys and jeans became popular. In the 1940s, during the war, fewer jeans were made. However, American soldiers used (put on) _____ jeans when they didn't have (wear) _____ their uniforms. In the 1950s jeans became popular with young people. They loved (wear) _____ them because jeans were a symbol of freedom. Movie stars like James Dean became famous (play) _____ tough anti-heroes in jeans and T-shirts. In the 1960s many university and college students chose (wear) _____ jeans. Different styles of jeans appeared and people in non-western countries, where jeans weren't sold, looked for ways (get) _____ them. Jeans soon seemed (be) _____ the common clothing for the new classless society.

In the 1970s, when jeans started (make) _____ in countries with low production costs, they became cheaper. More and more people wanted (have) _____ jeans. Even older people began (include) _____ them in their wardrobe. Jeans meant youth and everybody wanted (be) _____ young. In the 1980s famous designers decided (create) _____ their own style of jeans. They became high fashion. Jeans with holes in them appeared, made popular by Bon Jovi. Anti-fashion was in as well! Sales of jeans seemed (grow) _____ endlessly.

In the 1990s, during the worldwide recession, sales of jeans stopped (grow) _____ . But today jeans continue (be) _____ like old friends, practical and modern. Nobody can imagine jeans (be) _____ old-fashioned one day.

Unit 3 Forever young

3 Foreign languages? No, thank you.

Complete the text. Use *to*-infinitives and put in any missing words.

People in European countries often complain that most Britons don't want (speak) _____ a foreign language. It's easy (British people / communicate) _____ in their native language wherever they go, on holiday or on business.

They know that most foreigners have (learn) _____ English at school. And they expect (they / speak) _____ English well.

In 2003 the British government decided to allow (school children / give up) _____ _____ learning languages at the age of 14 if the children wanted to. The change was introduced in 2004 and today pupils are no longer forced (study) _____ a language to GCSE level. Since the introduction, the number of pupils who decide (do) _____ a GCSE in a foreign language has dropped to half the year group. Many education experts are disappointed and don't want (accept) _____ this decision. They think that Britain can't afford (make) _____ languages less important at school. In their opinion the government should encourage (pupils / study) _____ languages because they are needed in today's job market.

4 Forever young

Complete the table below using the words or phrases from the box. Add a few words about the new millennium and anything else you know about these decades.

ABBA • AIDS • American civil rights movement • baseball caps • the Beatles • break-dancing • Chernobyl disaster • Cold War • disco fever • economic crisis • Elvis • flared trousers • flower power movement • Gorbachev • Goth music • growing economy • hip hop • hippies • hot pants • James Dean • John Travolta • leggings • miniskirts • parkas • piercings • punks • rap • reunification of Germany • rock 'n' roll • the Rolling Stones • skateboarders • tattoos • techno • tight jeans • time after World War II • yuppies

	Political background, important events	People	Fashion, music and dancing
the 1950s	*time after World War II*	*Elvis, James Dean*	
the 1960s			
the 1970s			
the 1980s			
the 1990s			
the new millennium			

5 True or false?

Decide if these statements are true or false and explain why.

1. As a teenager, Kelly Osbourne didn't have a normal relationship with her dad.

   This statement is _____ because it says in the text that _____
   _____ .

2. In the 1950s parents weren't pleased about their kids wearing T-shirts and jeans.

   That's _____ because it says in the text that _____
   _____ .

3. In the 1960s unemployment was a big problem.

   That's _____ because the text says that _____
   _____ .

4. The punks of the 1970s were popular with everybody.

   This statement is _____ because the text says that _____
   _____ .

5. In the 1980s people had to face difficult situations.

   That's _____ because it says in the text that _____
   _____ .

6. The hip-hop generation copied the hippies of the 1970s.

   This statement is _____ because the text says that _____ .

6 Hair colour

Put the words in brackets into the correct form and add any missing words.

Hair-dying* has been popular with young people for several years. Girls prefer (buy) _____ purple and red dyes, boys prefer green and yellow. But why do people colour their hair?

Adam, 16: (His hair is green and pink.) When you're young, you're allowed (experiment) _____ . If I went to a job interview with coloured hair, they would look at me and laugh. They wouldn't even let (I / hand in) _____ my application form. One day I'll have (put) _____ on a suit and go to work without coloured hair.

Sarah, 15: (Her hair is red.) I coloured my hair because I was bored with it. My mum allowed (I / colour) _____ it. She said I should (use) _____ hair dye that comes out after six washes. So I don't need (worry) _____ about it being dangerous. But I'm always (worry / get) _____ wet!

James, 17: (He has got blue hair.) It's fun. My girlfriend wanted (I / dye) _____ my hair. I know it's unnatural and I ought (keep) _____ my hair brown. But it'll grow out. And I probably (not / do) _____ it again.

Mary, 14: (Her hair was pink.) I wanted (be) _____ cool and was with a group of friends. My parents were shocked. They certainly wouldn't let (I / do) _____ it again.

*NEW: hair-dying – *Haarefärben*

7 Rebel Without a Cause

The film REBEL WITHOUT A CAUSE, which was made in 1955, is still a lot of people's favourite film, at least their favourite James Dean film. James Dean died young, but he still became a film legend. In REBEL, James Dean plays a teenage boy, Jim Stark, who gets into trouble. Jim seems to be lost in a world that doesn't understand him. He loves his parents although he struggles against his strong mother and his weak father. James Dean plays the role excellently. Natalie Wood plays Judy, a popular teenage girl. Judy loves her dad more than anything else in the world, but he has a rather distant manner and doesn't show his feelings. Judy protests by running away and staying out all night. At least Judy has parents at home. Plato, played by Sal Mineo, has nobody but the housekeeper because his parents are in Europe. When he finally gets a letter from his father, there is only a cheque in it, without a written message asking, 'How are you?'. The teens hang around and take part in dangerous races risking their lives. 'Why are we doing this?' Jim asks Buzz, the gang leader. 'I dunno, we gotta do something,' Buzz explains. Young people in post-war America were expected to show respect for their parents and teachers and to obey rules. The teens in REBEL don't accept these rules and are bored with their comfortable lives in the suburbs. The parents in the film don't know what to do. In the 1950s it was unusual for a film to concentrate on the situation of teenagers. Their problems may seem small compared to those of young people today, who often have to cope with drug problems, increasing violence or unemployment. James Dean, however, has become the symbol of young people struggling to find their place in this world. He was killed in a car crash in 1955, a month before REBEL came into the cinemas.

Benutze die Informationen aus Rebel Without a Cause *(‚Denn sie wissen nicht, was sie tun'), um folgende Aspekte auf Deutsch zu erläutern (stichpunktartige Antworten genügen, keine wörtliche Übersetzung nötig).*

1 *James Deans Rolle im Film:*

2 *Beziehung Jims zu seinen Eltern:*

3 *Judys Schwierigkeit mit ihrem Vater:*

4 *Judys Reaktion:*

5 *Grund, warum Plato von seinem Vater enttäuscht ist:*

6 *Erwartungen der Erwachsenen an Jugendliche nach 1945 (zwei):*

7 *Probleme der Jugendlichen heutzutage (drei):*

8 *Grund, warum Dean danach keine Filme mehr machte:*

8 Too much weight?

Fill in the correct form of the verbs in brackets. Don't forget the preposition where necessary.

One in five students is overweight. Many parents and teachers worry (overeat) _____ _____ in a generation that doesn't like (do / sports) _____ or (be / active) _____ .

When people were poor after the war, they had to concentrate (provide) _____ as much food for their families as they could. Today there is definitely no advantage (eat) _____ as much as you can. At work and at home, people sit for most of the day. At lunch or dinner, however, they still insist (eat) _____ like an athlete after a marathon – even though there's a danger (get) _____ seriously ill.

Children are especially keen (eat) _____ crisps, hamburgers and chocolate. When their parents suggest (jog) _____ in the afternoon, a lot of children say they'd rather (sit) _____ indoors and (play) _____ computer games. When their mother recommends (cycle) _____ to school by bike, most children say they prefer (go) _____ by car. Instead of (do) _____ sport every day, most children surf the internet after school. How can we succeed (make) _____ them keen (lose) _____ a few pounds?

9 Combine the sentences

Use the words in brackets to link the sentences.

Kevin managed to lose ten pounds. He told his friends how he did it.

1 Well, I cycle to school. I don't take the bus any more. (instead of)

_____

2 I walk the dog every night. I no longer complain about it to my parents. (without)

_____

3 I'm trying to live more healthily. So I drink lots of water instead of cola. (by)

_____

4 My best friend and I have started playing basketball in the evenings. I must admit that we have doubts about whether we will be able to do it for a long time. (despite)

_____
_____

5 I've started to train for a half marathon. Last year I just watched sports competitions on TV. (instead of)

_____
_____

6 My mum cooks tasty meals with less meat and more vegetables. She doesn't use as much oil and butter as she used to, either. (without)

_____
_____

7 I'd like to lose another ten pounds. That's much better than dreaming about big hamburgers. (instead of)

_____

Unit 3 **Forever young**

10 Find the words

Which words or phrases from Text 2 are being explained?

1 to spend a lot of time in a place: _____
2 a strong hat which protects your head: _____
3 a person who drives a car: _____
4 to like very much: _____
5 someone who always tells funny stories: _____
6 to look after: _____

11 What is true about Text 2?

Listen to the first part of Text 2 and tick (✓) the correct endings. Be careful, sometimes more than one ending is correct.

1 What Andy likes about the fire station …
  A ☐ are the fire trucks and their horns.
  B ☐ is that he needn't be there at the weekend.
  C ☐ is that he can watch firefighters sometimes.

2 When there's a gas leak at the hospital, …
  A ☐ Andy rushes there on his bike.
  B ☐ Andy wears a firefighter's uniform.
  C ☐ Andy helps the firefighters.

3 Among Andy's favorite activities is …
  A ☐ eating pizza.
  B ☐ listening to funny stories.
  C ☐ riding long distances on his bike.

4 Sandy and Barth Engert …
  A ☐ adopted Andy in Florida.
  B ☐ say it was love at first sight when they met Andy.
  C ☐ were afraid of the problems Andy would bring.

12 Look what you did to me

Fill in the missing words.

about • and • another • are • brain • brush • but • care • children • day • everyone • family • friends • he • his • if • in • just • look • lots • of • out • problems • school • such • the (x2) • things • this • to • until • when • worried

Andy was the second child that the Engert family adopted. _____ older sister Pam also came into the _____ by adoption. Now that Andy is _____ his mid-30s, Sandy and Barth are _____ that soon they might be too old to _____ after him, but they don't want _____ make his sisters responsible for him. _____ problem is that Andy can do _____ of things on his own, but _____ like any other 'normal' 12-year-old, he needs someone to take _____ _____ him. Andy probably wouldn't have had any _____ if his mother hadn't drunk alcohol _____ she was pregnant. Parts of Andy's _____ were damaged forever. There are some _____ he can do brilliantly and there _____ others which he will never understand, _____ as dividing numbers and remembering to _____ his teeth. The Engerts didn't know _____ when they adopted Andy. It wasn't _____ he was 22 that they saw a TV program _____ kids with FAS and discovered that _____ was just like one of these _____ . By then, Andy had already become _____ love of his home town, Winter Park in Florida. Everyone knows him and _____ is fond of him. He's such a nice _____ funny person that he has got _____ everywhere. Sometimes he does odd jobs, _____ most of the time he is _____ on his bicycle and ready for _____ adventure with the Winter Park firefighters. _____ only he could graduate from high _____ and become a real firefighter one _____ !

13 Error spotting

Read the short text below. In each line a word is missing. Mark the position where it belongs with an ◆ and write the correct word on the line.

> a • by • do •
> from • his • much •
> to • who

Andy would certainly become brilliant firefighter if people let him. _____
However, he has struggle against lots of prejudice. It takes him _____
half an hour to his homework if he has to divide or subtract _____
numbers, and he needs lots of help his parents. But if you talk _____
to him about fire trucks, you will soon discover how he knows _____
about them. You might even be puzzled the details he remembers _____
about the trucks. I'm sure that mother must regret what she has _____
done to this wonderful person, is a man who never gives up. _____

14 The Osbourne family

Fill in the correct form of the words in brackets. Be careful, sometimes you have to add a preposition.

At the end of the 1970s, Ozzy Osbourne (call) _____ the 'Prince of Darkness'. Unfortunately, the heavy metal legend (become) _____ addicted* to drugs and alcohol. In 2002 about 20 TV cameras (allow / film) _____

him and his crazy family 24 hours a day. There are three kids in the Osbourne family, but Aimee (decide / move) _____ out when the TV show (start) _____ . She (feel) _____ embarrassed by her strange family: two overweight kids, Jack and Kelly, a crazy old heavy metal star father and his wife and business partner, Sharon. There is also an awful dog called Lola who can't (avoid / leave) _____ behind things we had better not mention. The Osbournes (live) _____ in a million-dollar villa and they (behave) _____ very strangely. Although they would never (apologize / use) _____ four-letter words*, they often (feel like / have) _____ long conversations with each other. All kinds of problems (discuss) _____ and (solve) _____ . This crazy household (name) _____ the most famous TV family of all time. The show (finish) _____ in 2005, but the Osbournes (can / still / see) _____ on our screens. Daughter Kelly has had several songs in the charts and she (start / work) _____ for the BBC. Mum Sharon (appear) _____ on various talent shows in the UK and America. They are now one of the UK's richest families.

*NEW: addicted – *süchtig*; four-letter word – *Schimpfwort*

Unit 3 Forever young

15 The MTV story

Listen and fill in the correct information to complete the sentences.

1. MTV was launched in _____ and showed _____ and interviews with famous singers.
2. Since 1984 _____ have been given out by the channel.
3. Today's programmes are mostly reality shows and _____ aimed at _____ .
4. MTV has worked with stars like P. Diddy to encourage young people _____ and be more active.
5. Today you can watch MTV in different _____ all across the _____ .

16 Let's order tickets on the internet

You are in a hurry to finish your final exams because you are leaving soon after for a short holiday in London. Two of your best friends are coming with you. On the internet you have found some fantastic news. Your favourite rock band are performing in London during your stay. You've decided to write and ask for further information.

- which concert hall?
- price?
- Add two aspects of your own.
- tickets?
- pay by credit card or international transfer?

Write an e-mail of about 150 words to the tour manager. Use your exercise book.

17 A word chain

Fill in the correct words. The last letter of a word gives you the first letter of the next. The letters in the boxes with stars spell out a word.

1. A woman who is having a baby soon is … .
2. TS makes a person produce a strange noise and a … .
3. to make a person suffering from a disease healthy
4. having to do with the economy of a country or an area
5. the official list of the most successful pop songs
6. a sudden attack of illness
7. someone who travels to a place to find out about it
8. ›› quite
9. A … party has as its theme a past decade.
10. Andy does … jobs.
11. something that makes you unable to use a part of your body properly
12. a young, rich person from the city
13. It's … if you are talking about your secret love and he or she is standing behind you.
14. connected with design and layout (e.g. newspapers, books, websites)
15. the winner
16. ›› almost
17. a colour
18. you can see it at the seaside
19. a hen lays it

Solution: __ __ __ __ __ __ __ __
*12 *6 *17 *3 *4 *11 *13 *1

Wie gut kannst du diese Tätigkeiten?

- ✱ sehr gut
- ☐ ziemlich gut
- ☒ noch nicht so gut

Unit	Land und Leute Ich weiß einiges über …	Sprechen Ich kann …	Hören Ich kann …	Lesen Ich kann …	Schreiben Ich kann …
1	☐ Australien und die dortige Lebensart. ☐ die Geschichte der australischen Ureinwohner. ☐ Cathy Freeman. ☐ Neuseeland und seine Naturschönheiten. ☐ Abenteuerurlaub in Neuseeland. ☐ den *Flying-Doctor*-Dienst in Australien.	☐ die unterschiedlichen Zeitformen im richtigen Kontext verwenden. ☐ die Zeitformen im Passiv richtig anwenden. ☐ Umschreibungen für unbekannte Wörter finden. ☐ sportliche Aktivitäten beschreiben. ☐ sagen, welche Gefühle ich empfinde. ☐ Landkarten beschreiben.	☐ das Unterrichtsgespräch verstehen. ☐ den Hörtexten im Schülerbuch und im Workbook folgen. ☐ Sprecher/innen mit australischem Akzent verstehen. ☐ Landkarten einem Hörtext entsprechend vervollständigen. ☐ Unterschiede zwischen dem Gesprochenen und dem Geschriebenen erkennen.	☐ Webseiten verstehen. ☐ Abkürzungen verstehen. ☐ Tagebucheinträge verstehen. ☐ Romantexte verstehen, auch wenn ich nicht alle Wörter kenne. ☐ Fragen zu Lesetexten stichpunktartig auf Deutsch beantworten.	☐ formelle E-Mails an wichtige Personen schreiben, um meine Meinung mitzuteilen und diese begründen. ☐ kurze Geschichten mithilfe von Stichpunkten schreiben. ☐ unbekannte Wörter umschreiben. ☐ in informellen E-Mails meine Gefühle beschreiben. ☐ Beschwerdebriefe schreiben.
2	☐ mögliche Entwicklungen in der Zukunft. ☐ intelligente Roboter. ☐ Wunderkinder. ☐ globale Erwärmung. ☐ den Regenwald und seine Zerstörung. ☐ das *Eden Project* in Cornwall. ☐ frühere Erwartungen an die Zukunft. ☐ das Buch *The Hitchhiker's Guide to the Galaxy*.	☐ für jemanden dolmetschen. ☐ Konjunktionen richtig benutzen, um Sätze zu verknüpfen. ☐ ausdrücken, was unter bestimmten Bedingungen … 1 als logische Folge geschieht. 2 geschehen wird oder kann. 3 geschehen würde oder könnte. 4 hätte geschehen können oder sollen. ☐ Bedürfnisse ausdrücken.	☐ Radioreportagen verstehen. ☐ nach dem Zuhören Fragen beantworten. ☐ Nachrichtensendungen auswerten.	☐ Leserbriefe verstehen. ☐ Partizipialkonstruktionen verstehen, die 1 einen Grund, 2 zeitliche Zusammenhänge, 3 Relativsätze wiedergeben. ☐ Fehler in Textzusammenfassungen finden. ☐ mit Vorsilben gebildete neue Wörter verstehen. ☐ Romanauszüge aus dem Genre Science-Fiction verstehen.	☐ kurze Leserbriefe schreiben. ☐ Briefe an eine Organisation schreiben und um Informationen bitten.

3

- die Entwicklung der Jugendkultur.
- Mode, Musik und Politik von den 1950er-Jahren bis heute.
- ☐☐ Möglichkeiten, sich fit zu halten.
- die Situation von Menschen mit unterschiedlichen Krankheiten.
- die Friedensbewegung.

- Verben + *to-infinitive* und Verben + *ing*-Form richtig verwenden.
- die Konstruktion Verb + Objekt + Infinitiv verwenden.
- *True* und *false friends* richtig verwenden.
- Verben, Adjektive und Nomen + Präposition + *ing*-Form richtig verwenden.
- mit verschiedenen Redemitteln über Hobbys und Interessen sprechen.

- einem Radiobericht eines DJ folgen.
- einem Hörtext entsprechend ein Anmeldeformular ausfüllen.

- Webseiten auswerten.
- einige englische Redewendungen verstehen.
- Texte in Tabellenform auswerten.
- beim Korrekturlesen fehlende Wörter erkennen und richtig einsetzen.
- Fragen den richtigen Textabschnitten zuordnen.

- kurze Texte über die Interessen und Probleme der heutigen Jugendlichen schreiben.
- auf Deutsch Zusammenfassungen von Texten erstellen.
- über eigene Hobbys und Interessen in der für Webseiten üblichen Form schreiben.
- Tickets über das Internet bestellen.
- Artikel für einen Wettbewerb schreiben.

4

- Land und Leute in Kanada.
- ☐☐ Toronto und seine Sehenswürdigkeiten.
- ☐☐ einen kanadischen Musiker.
- den lebensfeindlichen Norden Kanadas.
- die Kultur der Inuit.

- Aussagen durch Gradadverbien genauer formulieren.
- ausdrücken, was
  1 jemand hätte tun sollen.
  2 möglicherweise geschehen ist.
  3 höchstwahrscheinlich geschehen ist.
- ☐☐ Vorschläge machen.
- ☐☐ Vorschlägen zustimmen.
- ☐☐ Vorschläge ablehnen.
- ☐☐ jemanden zu etwas überreden.
- ☐☐ Vermutungen anstellen.
- ☐☐ meine Umgebung beschreiben.

- Sprecher/innen mit kanadischem Akzent verstehen.
- ☐☐ Beschreibungen Sehenswürdigkeiten zuordnen.
- Songs aus den internationalen Charts verstehen.
- zu Hörtexten gezielte Notizen machen.
- ☐☐ Berichte vervollständigen.
- ☐☐ Zusammenfassungen von Hörtexten schreiben.

- Songtexte lesen und verstehen.
- Tagebuchauszüge verstehen, auch wenn ich nicht alle Wörter kenne.
- authentische Texte über Sehenswürdigkeiten verstehen.

- meine Erfahrungen durch Adjektive mit positiven und negativen Bedeutungen näher beschreiben.
- E-Mails an Familienmitglieder schreiben, um meine Entscheidungen zu rechtfertigen.
- Tagebucheinträge schreiben.

Lern- und Arbeitstechniken:

Mir gelingt es, …

- ☐☐ die Wiederholung von Vokabeln für die Abschlussprüfung zu organisieren.
- ☐☐ neues Vokabular in vorhandene Mindmaps zu integrieren.
- ☐☐ unbekannte Wörter aus dem Kontext zu erschließen.
- ☐☐ grammatische Fragen mithilfe des Anhangs zu klären.
- ☐☐ meine Sprechfertigkeit zu perfektionieren.
- ☐☐ auf meinen Gesprächspartner / meine Gesprächspartnerin sinnvoll zu reagieren.

Wie kann ich besser werden?

Ich sollte …

- ☐☐ meine Vokabelkartei häufiger zur Wiederholung benutzen.
- ☐☐ alle unregelmäßigen Verben vor der Abschlussprüfung wiederholen.
- ☐☐ die wichtigsten Redewendungen für die drei Teile des Speaking Tests üben.
- ☐☐ die gesamte Grammatik wiederholen.
- ☐☐ meine Audio-CD genau anhören und Hörverständnisaufgaben üben.

18 Conspiracy theories

Find the correct tense and fill in the correct active or passive form of the verbs in brackets.

Do you really believe that Princess Diana and Dodi Al Fayed (die) _____ in a car accident in Paris in 1997? (Be) _____ it really an accident? Was she pregnant? Well, there are people who apparently (know) _____ more about her death. New theories (still / hit) _____ _____ the headlines and (frequent / appear) _____ on the internet. If you read them, you (soon / realize) _____ that the secret service (involve) _____ ! Did members of the royal family want (prevent / she / have) _____ a baby with a Muslim?

Did you know that the real Paul McCartney (kill) _____ in a car accident in 1966 and the person who (play) _____ Paul's part today, William Campbell, is just the winner of a lookalike* competition? What, you (not / believe) _____ this? Well, (can / prove*) _____ _____ the opposite? No? So you can see that Paul/William (do) _____ a brilliant job for over 40 years!

Since the invention of the internet there (be) _____ lots of conspiracy* theories like these. And what (make) _____ them so special is that we (not / can / they / prove) _____ wrong. However, neither (can / they / prove) _____ right.

One of these theories (seem) _____ quite amazing. (you / remember) _____ the deaths of the US Presidents Lincoln and Kennedy? Important aspects of their lives – and deaths – (be) _____ similar. Kennedy (elect*) _____ president in 1960. So (be) _____ Lincoln, except it was exactly a hundred years before, in 1860. Lincoln (shoot) _____ in the Ford Theatre and his killer (escape) _____ into a warehouse*. Kennedy's killer (wait) _____ in a warehouse in order to shoot the president as he drove by in a Ford Lincoln car. Afterwards he (hide) _____ in a theatre. Their killers both (come) _____ from the south of the USA and their names both had 15 letters: John Wilkes Booth and Lee Harvey Oswald. Both (kill) _____ soon after these murders. Do we have to mention that Kennedy's secretary (name) _____ Lincoln and Lincoln's secretary was – yes? – a Kennedy? And that both presidents (follow) _____ by a President Johnson – Andrew Johnson, born in 1808, and Lyndon B. Johnson, born in 1908 – and both Johnsons (die) _____ a decade after the murdered presidents?

Just chance? Well, yes. But if not – who (organize) _____ all of this?

*NEW: conspiracy – *Verschwörung*; lookalike – *Doppelgänger/in*; to prove – *beweisen*; to elect – *wählen*; warehouse – *Lager*

Unit 3 **Forever young**

19 How to Be Good

Find suitable questions (A–J) for the following parts of the extract on page 52 of your textbook. Be careful, you don't need all of the questions.

1 lines 1–7   _B_
2 lines 8–20   ____
3 lines 21–33   ____
4 lines 34–45   ____
5 lines 46–54   ____
6 lines 55–64   ____
7 lines 65–80   ____
8 lines 81–91   ____
9 lines 92–100 ____

A Who were the children's computers given to?
B What is the extract about?
C Why are the children in the women's refuge so poor?
D What was going on in the kitchen?
E Why didn't David ask his children?
F How did Katie and David celebrate Christmas?
G How did the children react to David's action?
H What did the children get for Christmas last year?
I What did David use to say when he refused to give his children a present?
J Who else could have helped the people in the women's refuge?

20 Who could have said this?

Fill in the first name of the correct member of the Carr family.

1 'I don't want to share it with my brother.' _____
2 'I can give you one of ours; our kids have got two, but they only need one.' _____
3 'I suppose we should help, but that's just too much!' _____
4 'One is enough for both of them. We have lots of other presents to buy.' _____

Key p. 45 — 12 points

21 Golders Green Fitness Centre

A London couple have just gone into Golders Green Fitness Centre to get some information about the centre and its courses. Listen and complete the form using the information you hear. You don't have to write complete sentences.

Golders Green Fitness Centre   Registration Form   132–134 Golders Green Road, Golders Green, London, NW11 8EF

1 Date: _____
2 Member's name: _William_____
3 Fitness problems: _has high blood pressure_ * _____
4 Advice: _____
5 Other courses: _yoga_____
   Time: _5:30 – 6:30_____
   Day: _____
6 Price: _____ _for 2 people_

Fitness adviser: _Sue Hunter_____
Other family members: _Linda (wife)_____
_____
_____
_exercise and swimming_____
_____
_____
_any day except Sunday_____

7 Member's phone number: _____

*NEW: blood pressure – Blutdruck

Key p. 45 — 10 points

CHECK OUT C

1 Choose the correct word from each box to fill the gaps. Be careful, there is one word in each box that you don't need.

> brilliant • embarrassing • fetal • political

1 It was so _____ ! I just couldn't remember her name!
2 He's a _____ young musician. He'll be big time in a few years.
3 She asked her teacher to explain the British _____ system to her.

> become • get • give • spends • treat

4 Andy's father never _____ any money on himself.
5 Lack of exercise has _____ a serious problem.
6 Some people refuse to _____ to charity.
7 Did Andy _____ a new bike for Christmas?

> art • meaning • opinion • way

8 What's your _____ of Andy's real mother?
9 What's the best _____ to help people with Tourette's Syndrome?
10 I don't know the exact _____ of 'FAS'.

2 Complete the second sentence so that it has a similar meaning to the first sentence. Use the word in the box. Do not change it. You must use between two and five words, including the word given.

1 Andy's mother had told him to be home by five o'clock, but he didn't remember. **forgot**
   Andy _____ home by five o'clock.
2 Andy can add and multiply, but he can't subtract numbers. **capable**
   Andy can add and multiply, but he _____ numbers.
3 Doctors told the Engerts, 'Why don't you look for a different baby?' **advised**
   Doctors _____ for a different baby.
4 Andy has always found reading very easy. **good**
   Andy has always _____ reading.
5 He just can't wait until his next birthday. **forward**
   He _____ his next birthday.

3 Guided writing

Write a short article of about 150 words for the NFC Radio competition. Look at the advert and find an answer to each of the problems and excuses.

> **NFC RADIO** Fitness – No, thanks?
>
> Fewer and fewer teenagers are interested in physical activities or doing sport. Here are some of their excuses:
>
> It's not cool.   I don't like teams.   I hate sport at school.
>
> No one in my family does it.   I'd rather play computer games.
>
> Enter our competition! Tell teenagers what they can do to improve their level of fitness in a short article with the title:
> **Fitness – No, thanks?**

20 points   Key p. 45

UNIT 4
CANADIAN MOSAIC

1 Canada quiz

Put a circle around the right answer. The correct letters give you the name of a Canadian city.

1 Canada is …
- ● the largest country in the world.   M
- ⊗ the second largest country in the world.   O
- ● as large as the USA.   V

2 What are Canada's official languages?
- ● English and Spanish   A
- ● French and Spanish   E
- ⊗ French and English   T

3 What is the capital city of Canada?
- ● Montreal   H
- ● Toronto   O
- ⊗ Ottawa   N

4 The most Asian city in North America is …
- ● Quebec City.   T
- ⊗ Vancouver.   R
- ● New York.   S

5 Most French-Canadians live in …
- ● Ontario.   E
- ⊗ Quebec.   O
- ● Manitoba.   B

6 Which modern game did Canada develop?
- ⊗ Ice hockey   T
- ● Badminton   R
- ● Baseball   L

Northwest Territories

City life in French-speaking Canada

Read the letters from 6 to 1. The name of the city is: T O R O N T O.

2 A crossword puzzle

Find the correct words or write the definitions.

Across

1 ~~To get~~ went over a road or river
3 to use something or to treat somebody unfairly
5 Alberta is one of ten Canadian …s.
7 the leaf of this tree is in the Canadian flag
9 the first people to live in the north of Canada

Crossword answers filled in:
1 across: GENERALLY
2 down: ENORMOUS
5 across: O U S
7 across: MAPLE
Down: DIVERS, HABIT

Down

2 _____
3 related to a racial, cultural or tribal group
4 _____
6 _____
8 a flat part of a plant

32 thirty-two

3 Sea Shepherd

Complete the text by putting in an adjective or an adverb.

Paul Watson is a Canadian environmentalist* who has become (international) _internationally_ known for his (tough) _tough_ methods to protect wildlife on the high seas. Born in Toronto in 1950, he grew up in New Brunswick. At the age of nine, he worked (hard) _hard_ to destroy the (cruel) _cruel_ animal traps he found in the forests. In 1968 he started his career as a seaman. Two years later he was a founding member of Greenpeace. After several years, he decided that Greenpeace didn't work (efficient) _efficiently_ enough. He left them in 1977 and founded his own organization, the Sea Shepherd* Conservation* Society.

Watson no longer jumped onto whaling ships to get into the news as he had done before. He (actual) _actually_ damaged and sank them because, in his opinion, they were weapons. The environmentalists worked (successful) _successfully_ : they saved thousands of whales and other sea animals. Watson's crew sank half the Icelandic whaling fleet and destroyed a whalemeat factory. They recorded (horrible) _horrible_ methods used in whale hunting and gave the tapes to the media. Although Watson has been in prison several times, he isn't (afraid) _afraid_ of continuing his work. He believes that his actions may seem (extreme) _extreme_ , but they stop (real) _real_ crimes. Sea Shepherd takes direct action where governments are unable or not (willing) _willing_ to make sure that conservation laws are obeyed. Watson thinks that we have to save the planet (urgent) _urgent_ . Lots of people support his actions. One famous supporter was the Crocodile Hunter, Steve Irwin. After his death, one of the ships was named after him.

*NEW: environmentalist – *Umweltschützer/in*; shepherd – *Hirte/Hirtin*; conservation – *Erhaltung, Schutz*

Paul Watson and Terri Irwin in front of the new ship

4 Word family search

Find words belonging to the same word family as the words in the box.

argument • crime • different • live • patient • reception • success

JAKSEMATESUCCEEDRFTCONPDISITYLAHEVRECEIVELZICEPATIENCETRAI
NJKLBDWEARDIFFERTERWILIFEURTMIORICRIMINALITTDERTRKPOTZANA
STUPVYSTUPPRSTARGUEPROSIMGSDVOJITOUPOSTELIVRATNYKSEMAUPVI

Unit 4 Canadian mosaic

5 Quebec

Complete the text by putting in an adjective or an adverb or by finding a suitable noun.

Quebec is Canada's largest ___city___ . It is seven times the ___kapital___ of the United Kingdom, but it has only seven million inhabitants. That's a quarter of Canada's _____ . Most Quebecers speak French, which has been the only (official) ___official___ language since 1974. Montreal and Quebec are the largest French-speaking cities in Canada. The French speakers have (strong) ___strong___ nationalist feelings. Lots of them think that Quebec should become (independent) ___independent___ because they would then be better able to protect the French _____ and culture.

In October 1995 the independence of Quebec from the rest of Canada seemed to be (possible) _____ . But then, in an (extreme) _____ close vote, more Quebecers chose to stay part of Canada rather than form their own _____ . Three days before the vote, tens of thousands of Canadians arrived in Montreal to take part in a demonstration. Some held _____ saying, 'We love Quebec – please don't go!' Most Canadians felt that a divided Canada would do less _____ with other countries. The Canadian _____ started to work to keep the country together. The 1999 opinion polls* (clear) _____ showed that fewer people supported an independent Quebec. In 2003 the pro-independence party was defeated once again.

*NEW: opinion poll – *Meinungsumfrage*

6 A weekend in Montreal

Anne has just returned to Boston after a weekend in Montreal. She is talking to Kevin. Add an adverb of degree. Pay attention to the number of stars.

> **Adverbs of degree**
> ★★★★ absolutely wonderful, totally ridiculous
> ★★★ very cold, really clever, extremely difficult, terribly slowly
> ★★ quite exciting, rather silly, fairly busy, pretty cool
> ★ a bit nervous, a little warmer

Kevin Hi, Anne. How was your weekend?

Anne It was lovely. It was (★★★) _____ exciting. Montreal is (★★★) _____ nice.

Kevin What did you do there?

Anne First my sister and I went shopping downtown. Montreal is a fashionable city, you know. In the evening we went to one of the many cool discos where we danced until the early morning. It was (★★★★) _____ fantastic.

Kevin That sounds (★★) _____ nice.

Anne Then on Sunday we visited the Olympic Park. It was built for the 1976 Summer Games and it's (★★★★) _____ amazing.

Kevin The Olympic Stadium is the home of Montreal's baseball team, the Expos.

Anne I know. We also went up the tower and had a (★★★) _____ fantastic view! Then we went to the Biodome right next door. There's a tropical rainforest inside.

Kevin Oh, that sounds (★★★) _____ interesting. Did you visit any of the museums? I know there are lots – about 30, I think.

Anne Just one. We went to Canada's oldest art museum. But my sister was (★) _____ bored, so we didn't stay long.

Kevin Did you get a chance to speak French?

Anne Yes, of course. I was (★) _____ nervous at first, but people could understand me (★★) _____ well.

7 An irritating person

Tick (✓) the correct answer and find the words in the text which show that it is right.

1 The Kellys live … A ☐ not far away from the city centre. B ☐ in downtown Toronto.

_____

2 Mrs Kelly is … A ☐ Steve's dad's brother. B ☐ Steve's mum's sister.

_____

3 When Karen compared the CN Tower and the Sears Tower, …
   A ☐ she didn't include the antenna. B ☐ she included the antenna.

_____

4 Mrs Kelly took a photo of Karen while she was …
   A ☐ lying on the floor of the CN Tower. B ☐ lying on the grass below the CN Tower.

_____

5 The Blue Jays once …
   A ☐ won the world championship. B ☐ were second only to a US baseball team.

_____

6 Steve … A ☐ prefers Canada to the US. B ☐ thinks Canada is inferior to the US.

_____

7 Quite a lot of movies that are set in New York City are filmed in Toronto because …
   A ☐ Toronto is culturally and ethnically a more diverse city.
   B ☐ New York is dirtier and a more dangerous place.

_____

8 Water freezes at … A ☐ 32° Fahrenheit. B ☐ at 0° Fahrenheit.

_____

8 The right word

Complete the sentences by using a word from the box.

> about • as (x2) • for •
> of (x2) • out • to

1 Karen regards Steve _____ a pretty irritating kind of person.
2 She pointed _____ that the CN Tower was taller.
3 CN stands _____ 'Canadian National'.
4 Steve couldn't think _____ a smart reply.
5 Karen reminded Steve _____ the time when the Blue Jays became world champions.
6 Steve was too polite to say _____ his hosts that he thought the US was the real thing.
7 They often talked _____ guns and crime.
8 Toronto is described _____ culturally and ethnically the most diverse city in the world.

Unit 4 Canadian mosaic

9 Short answer questions

Read the information and answer the questions. Do not use more than five words in each answer. You don't have to write complete sentences.

BLACK CREEK PIONEER VILLAGE

A visit to Black Creek Pioneer Village is a step back in time to 19th-century Ontario. 40 authentically restored homes, workshops, public buildings and farms recreate the atmosphere of life in a rural Victorian community of the 1860s. Craftspeople and workers wearing period costumes demonstrate skills such as open-hearth cooking, bread-making, looming, milling, blacksmithing, sewing, printing and more. Walk through the village and into the homes and buildings, visit the inn, and stroll through farms and forests. The Hands on History Centre lets kids try their hand at traditional trades and pioneer survival skills like building a log cabin or weaving cloth. During the holiday season in November and December, the village offers many special events to celebrate Christmas as it was 130 years ago.

The brand new Event Pavilion has opened the doors to a host of possibilities for Black Creek Pioneer Village. The covered pavilion includes a stage, seating for up to 300 people and a snack bar. Last year it was home to the Métis Arts Festival and the Celtic Sounds Festival.

Admission: Groups (min. 20 people) – 15% discount; Adults (ages 16–59) – $13 (GST incl); Children (ages 5–15) – $9 (GST incl); Seniors (60+) – $12 (GST incl); Students (16+ with ID) – $12 (GST incl); Family annual membership: $85

1. Which period is recreated in the Black Creek Pioneer Village? _____
2. What can you see as well as buildings? _____
3. What can children learn at the Hands on History Centre? _____
4. What can people do in the new Event Pavilion? Name two activities. _____
5. How much are the tickets for a family of two adults and two children aged 4 and 12? _____

10 The great sled race

Complete the text by putting the words in brackets into the correct form or by adding a word.

The Yukon Quest International Sled* Dog Race (cover) _____ 1,000 miles or 1,600 kilometres between Fairbanks, Alaska, and Whitehorse, Canada, (change) _____ direction every year. Since 1984 this tough sled dog race (become) _____ more and more popular. The Yukon Quest trail follows the old mail routes and Gold Rush trails (create) _____ over a hundred years ago. The teams have to climb three mountains and travel hundreds of miles over the (freeze) _____ rivers of the north. The sleds are (heavy) _____ loaded with food, clothing and camping equipment. There may be dangers such _____ wild animals, blizzards and (terrible) _____ cold weather. Training a dog team, usually made up of huskies or qimmiqs, is (hard) _____ work and (take) _____ a lot of time and attention all year.

*NEW: sled – Schlitten

11 Here comes the qimmiq!

Rewrite these sentences and change the nouns into adverbs, adverbs into adjectives and so on.

1 There is no doubt that the qimmiq, or the Inuit sled dog, is perfect for dog races.

 The qimmiq is _undoubtedly perfect for dog races_____.

2 Certainly, lots of people choose the qimmiq for sled dog races because of its ability to pull 150 per cent of its own weight over great distances.

 It is _____ that lots of people _____

 because it _____ of its own weight over great distances.

3 Traditionally there are eleven dogs in a team.

 In a _____ team there are eleven dogs.

4 In general, the dogs need twelve days to get from Whitehorse in the Yukon to Fairbanks, Alaska.

 The dogs _____ to get from Whitehorse to Fairbanks, Alaska.

5 The excited sled dogs will run 1,000 miles (1,600 kilometres) across the ice.

 The sled dogs will run _____ miles across the ice.

6 It's no surprise to hear that you can't use a cellphone out there.

 You _____ that you can't use a cellphone out there.

7 But most competitors are happy to accept temperatures of up to minus 50 degrees Celsius at night.

 Temperatures of up to _____

 _____.

12 Fill in can / could / might / must / should + have + past participle

Harriet Where's my cellphone? I can't find it, I (leave) _____ it somewhere.

Mom Well, you (take) _____ it to school even though I told you to leave it at home.

Harriet But I (not / lose) _____ it because I'm always very careful with it.

Mom Oh I see! May I remind you of what happened to your old cellphone? We really (not / give) _____ you a new one so quickly!

Harriet That's not fair! I know my new phone was on my desk this morning! Jamie (take) _____ it!

Mom Definitely not. Your little brother (not / do) _____ it because he can't reach things on your desk.

Dad Harriet, here's your cellphone. I needed it to make some urgent business calls. What's the matter? Oh, I know, I (ask) _____ before using it. Next time, OK?

Unit 4 Canadian mosaic

13 In the middle of nowhere

Read these statements about Text 2 and tick (✓) the correct box.

1 Cathy came from London.
2 Bob didn't like her.
3 Cathy and Bob were looking into a possible scandal.
4 The weather was going to change for the worse.
5 Cathy was very tired on her journey into nowhere.
6 Most Canadians live in the north of the country.
7 There are lots of disadvantages for the Inuit.
8 You can easily travel through the swamplands in summer.

	True	False	Not in text
1			
2			
3			
4			
5			
6			
7			
8			

14 Who said this?

The following sentences were said by the people in the box. Write the correct letter next to the sentence. Be careful, one sentence wasn't said by any of the people in the box.

> A Cathy McBride B Cathy's colleague Bob C a gas station attendant
> D a Winnipeg police officer E a man in the truck

1 'She was here some days ago, but she didn't stay long. After her phone call she ran to her car and drove on.'
2 'When we found the car, there was no one in it. The car wasn't damaged in any way.'
3 'The last time I spoke to her she was at a gas station.'
4 'Look what those men are doing! They must be dumping some drums. We'd better not stay around here. Let's try and catch another seal*.'
5 'Here is her camera. But there's no memory card in it. Well, let's take it anyway, and I'll take her diary and read it later.'
6 'My phone isn't working. Can I phone from here?'

*NEW: seal – *Robbe*

15 Dictionary work

The following words have various meanings. Which of the meanings given in the dictionary is the one used in Text 2? Underline the best German translation.

join (page 62, line 1)
(VERB) **1** *Teile usw.* verbinden, zusammenfügen
2 *jmdm.* Gesellschaft leisten
3 Mitglied werden, beitreten *to join the army Soldat werden*
4 join in mitmachen *Let's join in the singing! Lass uns mitsingen!*

lie (page 62, line 22)
(VERB) **1** lügen
2 liegen
3 *Friedhof* ruhen *Here lies the body of … . Hier ruht … .*
4 sich hinlegen Lie face down. *Leg dich auf den Bauch.*
(NOMEN) **5** Lüge

work (page 63, line 4)
(VERB) **1** arbeiten *We're working on it. Wir arbeiten daran.*
2 sich auswirken
3 *Maschine* funktionieren, laufen *My computer isn't working. Mein Computer geht nicht.*
4 etwas bedienen
(NOMEN) **5** Arbeit
6 *Kunst usw.* Werk

sign (page 63, line 23)
(VERB) **1** *Vertrag, Dokument usw.* unterschreiben, unterzeichnen
2 unter Vertrag nehmen
(NOMEN) **3** Zeichen *to give a sign to sb jmdm. ein Zeichen geben*
4 Verkehrsschild *stop sign Stoppschild*
5 Anzeichen, Spur
6 *Astrologie* Sternzeichen

38 thirty-eight

16 A closed police file

Listen to the police officer talking to his secretary and complete the police report form.

Winnipeg Police Service　　　　　　　　　　　　　　　File number: _____

Surname: _McBride_____　　　Nationality: _____

First name: _____　　　　Employer: _Manitoba Mirror_____

Events: _Investigated a story at the end of_ _____

Contacted her colleague by _____ _and_ _____ _at gas station_

Followed a 12-tonne truck carrying more than 50 _____

Reporter suspected truck was probably carrying dangerous _____ _waste_

Disappeared soon afterwards somewhere in the _____ _north of Winnipeg_

Reporter's car was found _____

Cathy McBride probably had an _____

File closed: _____27_____

17 Find the questions

how • where (x3) • when • which • who • why (x2)

be • call (x2) • come • get • go • spend

It's Friday night. You are late and your parents have some annoying questions for you. Choose a question word and a verb from the boxes and use the words in brackets to complete the dialogue.

1 Finally, you're here! Just tell us, dear, (should) _____ home?
   – Well, at half past ten, I know, but … .

2 (not) _____ to tell us that you'd be late?
   – Well, I left my cellphone at home and … .

3 And _____ , by the way?
   – I was at the school disco, you know that.

4 No, you weren't. We've just phoned Rachel and she told us that you left the disco hours ago. _____ ?
   – Oh, did she? Well, I just went to a pub downtown to see if Johnny was there.

5 Johnny? _____ Johnny? And _____ there if I may ask?
   – A friend of ours had his motorbike with him and … .

6 What? He took you on his motorbike? I can't believe it! And _____ is this Johnny?
   – He is our new tennis instructor at school and … .

7 But _____ him by his first name if he's your teacher?
   – That's because my friend Rachel … .

8 Leave it, just leave it, we don't want to hear any more tall stories. But I can tell you one thing: _____ every weekend for the rest of this school year?
   – At home.

Unit 4 Canadian mosaic

18 What would you have done?

This is Aron Ralston, an experienced US sportsman who gave up a career in engineering to spend more time in his favourite place – outdoors in the middle of nowhere. He's the author of *Between a Rock and a Hard Place* and is now known around the world. Complete this text about him.

Aron is known for his courage. He narrowly escaped death in May 2003. If he (not / leave) _____ for a solo day trip in the Bluejohn Canyon, Utah, he (miss) _____ the greatest challenge of his life – something he possibly (not / regret) _____ ! If Aron (not / try) _____ to climb down a dangerous ravine in the remote canyon, an enormous piece of rock (not / fall) _____ down those narrow canyon walls without attracting any attention. But this 350-kilo rock trapped him. His family and friends (do) _____ anything to rescue him if they (know) _____ that his right arm had got stuck under that rock. But he hadn't told anyone where he was going. What a mistake!

After five long days and cold nights out there in the middle of nowhere, Aron was not very strong. But he realized that he (have to / cut) _____ off his arm if he (want) _____ to save his life. He then broke the bones in his arm and cut it off below the elbow* using a pocket knife. This 'operation' (take) _____ him ages if he (not / be) _____ in so much pain. But he hurried and it 'only' took him an hour. Aron then walked on through the canyon until a rescue helicopter found him. He certainly (not / survive) _____ if he (not / have) _____ so much courage. No one could imagine what he'd been through. And even if he (not / appear) _____ on TV shows, he (remember) _____ by every US citizen. If you (be) _____ interested in finding out more about Aron, you (find) _____ lots of articles on the internet.

*NEW: elbow – *Ellbogen*

19 A trip to the Bluejohn Canyon

You are travelling round Canada and the States and you are planning a trip to the Bluejohn Canyon. Unfortunately your parents have heard about what happened to Aron Ralston and they are trying to keep you from experiencing the greatest challenge of your life.

However, you are determined to go and so you decide to send them an e-mail of about 150 words. Write in your exercise book. Tell them …

- who you are going with;
- how long you'll be there;
- what could go wrong and how you're preparing to prevent this (three aspects);
- why taking this challenge is so important to you;
- and add two aspects of your own.

20 Diary of a South African

Find the explanations which fit the words in bold as used in the text.
Tick (✓) the correct box. Be careful, sometimes more than one answer is correct.

1 **I shovelled snow** for the first time … . (line 13)
  A ☐ I lifted and moved snow … .
  B ☐ I saw snow … .
  C ☐ I walked in the snow … .

2 … **the temperature dropped to around minus 20°C**. (lines 22–23)
  A ☐ … the temperature wasn't lower than 20°C.
  B ☐ … the temperature fell to minus 20°C.
  C ☐ … it became colder than before.

3 **More snow and ice is expected**. (lines 34–35)
  A ☐ There will be snow and ice except in this area.
  B ☐ There will be more snow and ice very soon.
  C ☐ The bad conditions won't be over soon.

4 **Not a tree or a bush** in the garden **that hasn't been damaged**. (lines 44–45)
  A ☐ All the plants in the garden have been damaged.
  B ☐ None of the trees and bushes have been damaged.
  C ☐ There is no bush or tree that is still undamaged.

5 **The power is** still **off**. (line 63)
  A ☐ The electricity will be turned off soon.
  B ☐ There will be no electricity in the next few days.
  C ☐ The electricity isn't working at the moment.

6 … the bastard **got away**. (line 70)
  A ☐ … he managed to leave.
  B ☐ … he was able to escape.
  C ☐ … he was very surprised.

10 points | Key p. 46

21 Police Constable Wang

17 You and your little sister are listening to a radio interview about immigrants to Canada. As your sister can only understand part of the interview, she wants to know:

- what we learn about Wang and his family;
- what jobs he has had in the last four years;
- where he got the idea of becoming a policeman from;
- why his native language helps him in his job;
- if Wang is the only immigrant in the Toronto Police Service.

Listen and take notes on a piece of paper. Then write a summary of the interview in German. Write about 120 words.

_____
_____
_____
_____
_____
_____
_____
_____
_____

10 points | Key p. 46

CHECK OUT D

1 Say it in other words.

Bob hasn't heard from Cathy (recently) _____¹ and is starting to get worried. He's tried (to call) _____² her and left (some) _____³ messages, but she hasn't (replied) _____⁴ yet. Cathy (generally) _____⁵ keeps him informed about all of her actions. The Manitoba swamplands are (very large) _____⁶ and Cathy isn't used to the (really) _____⁷ inhospitable (environment) _____⁸. They've got some information about a chemical (factory) _____⁹ which is about to be (closed) _____¹⁰ down because of low safety standards.

2 Complete the second sentence so that it has a similar meaning to the first sentence. The start of the new sentence has been given.

1 Cathy didn't ask a colleague to go into the swamplands with her.

   Cathy should have _____.

2 Surely the two men killed her.

   She must _____.

3 Bob told the police that Cathy was a fast but careful driver.

   Bob told the police that Cathy drove _____.

4 The police needed several days to find Cathy's car.

   It took _____.

5 It's been nearly a year since Bob last saw Cathy.

   Bob hasn't _____.

3 Guided writing

Imagine you are on an exchange programme in Canada and you lose your way in Toronto while you are in the city centre.

When you finally get home, you write about your experience in your diary. Write around 150 words about what happened and mention the following:

☞ when and where it happened;
☞ your thoughts and feelings when you realized you were lost;
☞ ??? (Mention two additional aspects.)
☞ ???
☞ the end of your adventure.

42 forty-two

Key p. 46 | 20 points

CHECK ... Lösungen

UNIT 1 Check your reading

20 Grandmother `10 Punkte`

1 seine Mutter starb, Vater schickte Nachricht
2 mit Englisch aufgewachsen, kann auch Maori
3 wurde erwartet, dass sie sich an europäische Sitten anpassen (glaubten, nur so überleben zu können)
4 hatte harte Füße; war groß; roch unangenehm (hatte schwarze Haare; große Zähne; außergewöhnliche Hüte; war dick)
5 war sanft und hart zugleich
6 er sollte weggehen; etwas über sich selbst erfahren; heiraten falls nötig (genießen, was Städte und Menschen zu bieten haben; zurückkommen, wenn sie ihn dazu aufforderte)

➤ *Bei den Fragen 4 und 6 sind jeweils drei Punkte zu erreichen. Achte darauf, dass du, wie bei der Frage erwähnt, drei unterschiedliche Details auflistest. Ganze Sätze sind hier nicht nötig, aber ein Wort genügt nicht als Antwort.*

Ich habe ☐ von **10 Punkten erreicht.**

UNIT 1 Check your listening

21 The Crocodile Hunter `10 Punkte`

1 KSA Radio Service
2 killed by a stingray
3 filming a documentary
4 TV show with deadly animals; work with Australian wildlife
5 wife Terri also worked with him; had two children
6 was interesting; warm-hearted; cared about Australia and its wildlife

➤ *Lies die Fragen gründlich durch, damit du weißt, worauf du achten musst. Mache dir dann ausreichend Notizen, damit du anschließend die Fragen beantworten kannst.*

Ich habe ☐ von **10 Punkten erreicht.**

CHECK OUT A

1 Who or what is it? `10 Punkte`

1 champion
2 scary
3 farm labourer
4 glacier
5 receipt
6 outback
7 swimsuit
8 jack
9 Aborigines
10 rainforest

➤ *Wiederhole die Vokabeln auf den Seiten 123 bis 127. Hier findest du die gesuchten Wörter.*

2 Complete the text. `10 Punkte`

1 has been working
2 's/is going to stop
3 've/have known
4 was
5 taught
6 surfs
7 was carrying
8 'll/will have
9 'd/had put
10 was enjoyed

➤ *Einen Überblick über die* verb tenses *findest du auf den Seiten 100 bis 104 im Schülerbuch.*
Lies immer den kompletten Satz, nicht nur bis zur Lücke. Oft stehen am Satzende Zeitangaben, die dir helfen, die richtige Zeitform zu wählen. Übe mithilfe der EXERCISES 1, 2, 3, 13 und 14 im Schülerbuch.

3 Guided writing

(*Lösungsvorschlag*)
Dear Sir or Madam,
Last February I went on one of your tours that was advertised on the internet. Unfortunately my trip was quite different from the advert there, which mentioned that we would stay in comfortable first-class hotels. In three of the eight hotels the rooms were dirty and extremely small. And when we went round New Zealand by bus, the air conditioning wasn't working. It was over 40°C. The guidebooks we were given were free, but they were no use because they were out of date. One of the books was printed in 1980. Then the trip to Milford Sound couldn't take place because the bus had broken down. When we went to a museum near the hotel instead, we had to pay for the tickets, although it said in the advert that all entrance fees would be included.
Yours sincerely, Stefan Musterer

Bewertungstipps:
1 Inhalt: *Hast du über alle Punkte geschrieben, die als Anmerkung erwähnt sind, und auch den zusätzlichen Aspekt nicht vergessen? Dein Brief braucht auch eine Anrede und eine Schlussformel. Die Anmerkungen sind nicht sehr spezifisch. Lass dir etwas einfallen.*
2 Rechtschreibung und Grammatik: *Überprüfe mithilfe des Wörterverzeichnisses im Schülerbuch die Schreibung der Wörter, bei denen du unsicher bist, oder benutze ein Wörterbuch. Bei diesem Brief wirst du meistens das* simple past *benutzen, denn die Reise ist schon vorbei.*
3 Stil: *Versuche, Wiederholungen zu vermeiden und nicht zu unhöflich zu wirken, auch wenn du dich beschwerst.*

Ich habe ☐ von **20 Punkten erreicht.**

UNIT 1 und CHECK OUT A:
40–30: Klasse!
29–19: Ist OK!
Unter 19: Lies die Tipps und übe regelmäßig!

CHECK ... Lösungen

UNIT 2 Check your reading

20 The Hitchhiker's Guide ... [6 Punkte]

1 false
2 not in the text
3 true
4 false
5 false
6 not in the text

▶ Lies die Sätze gründlich durch und vergleiche sie mit den passenden Abschnitten im Text.

21 Finish the sentences. [4 Punkte]

1 for five or six years
2 to inform the people of Earth about the demolition of their planet
3 the plans had been on display for 50 years
4 getting a lift on a Vogon spaceship

▶ Der Satz muss natürlich grammatisch richtig sein.

Ich habe von 10 Punkten erreicht.

UNIT 2 Check your listening

22 Environmental issues ...

Part 1 [4 Punkte]
1 D 2 C 3 – 4 – 5 B 6 A

▶ Es ist nicht schlimm, wenn du nicht jedes Wort verstehst. Achte darauf, ob irgendwelche Schlüsselwörter zu den angeführten Themenbereichen erwähnt werden.

Part 2 [6 Punkte]
7 B 8 A; C 9 A; B 10 B

▶ Lies dir die Satzanfänge und die Auswahlmöglichkeiten sorgfältig durch, damit du weißt, worauf du achten musst. Bei diesem Aufgabentyp können auch mehrere Lösungen korrekt sein.

Ich habe von 10 Punkten erreicht.

CHECK OUT B

1 Find the correct nouns. [10 Punkte]

1 necessity
2 scientists
3 importance
4 knowledge
5 success
6 solution
7 trial
8 business
9 competitors
10 attractions

▶ Wiederhole die Wörter auf den Seiten 128 bis 132. Achte auch auf die Informationen in der roten Spalte.

2 Complete the text. [10 Punkte]

1 hadn't looked
2 wouldn't have seen
3 take
4 will notice
5 put
6 takes
7 had realized
8 wouldn't have left
9 was
10 wouldn't steal

▶ Einen Überblick über Bedingungssätze findest du auf den Seiten 107 und 108 im Schülerbuch. Lies zunächst den gesamten Text, damit du die zeitlichen Zusammenhänge verstehst. Überlege dann, welcher Satztyp am besten passt. Übe mithilfe der EXERCISE 14 im Workbook.

3 Guided writing

(*Lösungsvorschlag*)
Hi Ryan,
I'm writing this e-mail on my new notebook. I got it for my birthday last Friday. My dad took me to Computer Paradise and we tested all the computers there. Then we decided to buy this one. You know my old computer was rubbish. It kept switching itself off, and that happened three times a day sometimes. My new notebook is very light, so I can take it everywhere. And I can surf on the internet wherever I want – even in the garden! But I normally use it to do my written homework.
Another good thing is that I can take it to my room to watch DVDs. You know, my old computer didn't have a DVD drive. Now my little sister wants my old computer, but she can have it. It doesn't work anyway.
Bye for now, Alex

Bewertungstipps:
1 Inhalt: *Hast du über alle Punkte geschrieben, die als Anmerkung erwähnt sind, und auch die zwei zusätzlichen Aspekte nicht vergessen? Deine E-Mail braucht auch eine Anrede und eine Schlussformel.*
2 Rechtschreibung und Grammatik: *Überprüfe mithilfe des Wörterverzeichnisses im Schülerbuch die Schreibung der Wörter, bei denen du unsicher bist, oder benutze ein Wörterbuch.*
Bei dieser E-Mail musst du sowohl die present tenses *als auch die* past tenses *benutzen.*
3 Stil: *Versuche, einen zusammenhängenden Text zu schreiben. Wörter wie* then, and, but, another good thing *und* now *verbessern den Stil. Denke daran, dass du an eine/n Freund/in schreibst. Die Sprache soll nicht zu förmlich sein.*

Ich habe von 20 Punkten erreicht.

UNIT 2 und CHECK OUT B:
40–30: Kompliment!
29–19: Nicht schlecht!
Unter 19: Lies die Tipps!

CHECK ... Lösungen

UNIT 3 Check your reading

19 How to Be Good `8 Punkte`

1 B 2 D 3 G 4 E 5 H 6 A 7 J 8 I 9 C

➤ *Vorsicht! Eine Frage bleibt übrig.*

20 Who could have said this? `4 Punkte`

1 Molly   3 Tom
2 David   4 Katie

➤ *Die Aussagen stehen so nicht wörtlich im Text, aber es gibt viele Hinweise.*

Ich habe von **12 Punkten erreicht.**

UNIT 3 Check your listening

21 Golders Green Fitness Centre `10 Punkte`

1 13th February
2 Wigglesworth
3 wants to lose weight; feels tired most of the time
4 fitness test
5 Thursday; aqua aerobics; 12:45–1:30
6 £ 179.99
7 020 607 21461

➤ *Lies das Formular genau durch, damit du dich auf die gesuchten Informationen konzentrieren kannst. Schreibe auf jeden Fall, was du gehört hast, auch wenn es z.B. nur die Hälfte der Telefonnummer ist. Beim zweiten Anhören kannst du dann den Rest sicher ergänzen.*

Ich habe von **10 Punkten erreicht.**

CHECK OUT C

1 Choose the correct word. `10 Punkte`

1 embarrassing   6 give
2 brilliant   7 get
3 political   8 opinion
4 spends   9 way
5 become   10 meaning

➤ *Überfliege zunächst alle Sätze, bevor du beginnst, die Lücken zu füllen.*
Denke daran, dass es sowohl true *als auch* false friends *gibt.*

2 Complete the sentence. `10 Punkte`

1 forgot to come
2 isn't capable of subtracting
3 advised the Engerts to look
4 been good at
5 is looking forward to

➤ *Wenn alles richtig ist, bekommst du zwei Punkte pro Satz. Wenn nur die Hälfte richtig ist, bekommst du einen Punkt. Lies zunächst den Ausgangssatz. Schaue dir dann das Wort an und überlege, was du über das Wort weißt. Folgt nach dem Wort eine -ing-Form oder ein to-infinitive? Sind bestimmte Präpositionen mit dem Wort verbunden? Überprüfe am Schluss, ob dein neuer Satz mit dem Ausgangssatz bedeutungsgleich ist.*

3 Guided writing

(*Lösungsvorschlag*)
Fitness – No, thanks?
So you are not interested in sport and always find excuses to avoid physical activities? Perhaps you think that doing sport is not cool. But have you thought about sports stars like David Beckham or Lukas Podolski who earn lots of money and are very cool?
If no one in your family likes sport, you should be the first. Maybe the others will follow your example. If you hate team sports, there are lots of sports you can do on your own or with a friend, like cycling for example. Some of you prefer playing computer games, and that's easy to understand, but if you plan carefully, you can do both and be a lot fitter. And if you hate sport at school, why not talk to your teacher? They might have an alternative activity that you'll like. There's always hope, just keep trying and don't give up!

Bewertungstipps:
1 Inhalt: *Hast du alle Ausreden und Probleme berücksichtigt? Versuche, einen möglichst zusammenhängenden Text zu verfassen und entsprechende Gegenargumente zu formulieren. Konntest du 150 Wörter schreiben?*
2 Rechtschreibung und Grammatik: *Bei dieser Art von Text wirst du häufig* if-*Sätze und Hilfsverben wie* should *oder* might *verwenden. Es geht hier darum, Ratschläge zu geben.*
3 Stil: *Denke daran, dass du einen Artikel schreibst. Bemühe dich, nicht zu förmlich zu schreiben, denn die Adressaten sind Jugendliche.*

Ich habe von **20 Punkten erreicht.**

UNIT 3 und CHECK OUT C:
42–30: Klasse!
29–19: In Ordnung!
Unter 19: Lies die Tipps und übe regelmäßig. Es bleibt nicht mehr viel Zeit bis zur Prüfung!

CHECK ... Lösungen

UNIT 4 Check your reading

20 Diary of a South African `10 Punkte`

1 A 2 B; C 3 B; C 4 A; C 5 C 6 A; B

▶ *Denke daran, dass es manchmal mehr als eine richtige Lösung gibt.*

Ich habe von 10 Punkten erreicht.

UNIT 4 Check your listening

21 Police Constable Wang `10 Punkte`

(*Lösungsvorschlag*)
Wang ist ein junger chinesischer Einwanderer, der kanadischer Staatsbürger ist. / Er ist verheiratet und hat eine kleine Tochter. / Zurzeit arbeitet er bei der Polizei in Toronto.
Bevor er Polizist wurde, studierte er Informatik, gab jedoch sein Studium auf, / lieferte chinesisches Essen aus und betrieb ein eigenes Restaurant. /
Auf die Idee, Polizist zu werden kam er durch einen Artikel in einer chinesischsprachigen Zeitung / und eine Fernsehsendung, in der man Chinesen suchte, die sich für eine Stelle bei der Polizei von Toronto interessierten. /
Seine Sprachkenntnisse kommen ihm in seinem Beruf oft zugute, denn er muss dolmetschen / oder seinen Kollegen helfen, die kein Chinesisch sprechen. /
Wang ist einer von vielen Einwanderern, / bei ihm auf der Arbeit werden 29 verschiedene Sprachen gesprochen.

▶ *Du musst fünf Aspekte erwähnen und bekommst dafür zwei Punkte pro Aspekt. Das Zeichen / gibt an, wie die Punkte verteilt sind. Am besten machst du deine Notizen zunächst auf Englisch, dann verlierst du beim Zuhören keine Zeit mit dem Übersetzen. Hinterher kannst du dann in Ruhe deine Zusammenfassung auf Deutsch formulieren.*

Ich habe von 10 Punkten erreicht.

CHECK OUT D

1 Say it in other words. `10 Punkte`

1 lately
2 to phone
3 several
4 answered
5 usually
6 enormous
7 extremely
8 surroundings
9 plant
10 shut

▶ *Lies zunächst den ganzen Satz, bevor du beginnst, die Lücken zu füllen.*

2 Complete the sentence. `10 Punkte`

1 asked a colleague to go into the swamplands with her
2 have been killed by the two men
3 fast but carefully
4 several days for the police to find Cathy's car
5 seen Cathy for nearly a year

▶ *Wenn alles richtig ist, bekommst du zwei Punkte pro Satz. Wenn nur die Hälfte richtig ist, bekommst du einen Punkt. Lies zunächst den Ausgangssatz. Schaue dir dann den Satzanfang an und überlege, wie der gesuchte Satz sinngemäß lauten könnte. Überprüfe am Schluss, ob dein neuer Satz mit dem Ausgangssatz bedeutungsgleich ist.*

3 Guided writing

(*Lösungsvorschlag*)
Guess what happened this afternoon? Mike and I went to the Eaton Centre in Toronto. I left Mike to look for a DVD shop and then went outside the shopping centre to find some other shops. I spent almost an hour looking around and then I suddenly remembered that I had to meet Mike in three minutes! But I couldn't remember how to get back. I was extremely worried and ran through several streets in a complete panic! I thought about phoning Mike, but remembered that he had left his cellphone at home. Suddenly I saw a friendly policeman and asked him for help. The problem was that I couldn't remember the name of the shopping centre. So I described the building to him and he actually knew where I wanted to go. He showed me the way and when I got to the entrance, Mike was waiting for me patiently.

Bewertungstipps:
1 Inhalt: *Hast du alle Anregungen berücksichtigt und zwei eigenen Aspekte erwähnt? Lass dir etwas Passendes einfallen. Zähle schnell nach, ob du ca. 150 Wörter geschrieben hast. In der Abschlussprüfung musst du auch ca. 150 Wörter schreiben.*
2 Rechtschreibung und Grammatik: *Bei dieser Art von Text musst du häufig Vergangenheitsformen wie* simple past *und* past perfect *verwenden. Die Ereignisse haben schon stattgefunden.*
3 Stil: *Bemühe dich, klar und verständlich zu schreiben. Denke daran, dass du in deinem Tagebuch schreibst, also achte auf einen informellen Stil.*

Ich habe von 20 Punkten erreicht.

UNIT 4 und CHECK OUT D:
40–30: Toll!
29–19: Nicht schlecht!
Unter 19: Teile die Zeit gut ein und übe regelmäßig mithilfe der Tipps! Es sind nur noch ein Paar Wochen bis zur Prüfung.

Whale Rider

NACH UNIT 1

1 The story begins with the birth of Paikea, or Pai for short, and the death of her twin brother and mother. 'When I was born,' says Pai, 'my twin brother died and took our mother with him.' Her father goes off
5 to Europe and leaves Pai growing up with her grandparents.

Grandfather Koro is deeply disappointed about the birth of a granddaughter. He is the village chief, the last leader in a line that goes back to another Paikea,
10 the tribe's ancestor. Maori stories say that Paikea arrived in New Zealand on the back of a whale a millennium ago. —A—

Koro can't accept that Pai might become chief because she is female. 'She won't be of any use to
15 me,' he says. Grandmother Flowers doesn't share his opinion. 'The old paka thinks he knows everything about being a chief,' she says. She is a warm-hearted and wise woman. She holds the family together. —B—

20 When Pai gets older, she is determined to earn her grandfather's respect. The girl shares his love of Maori traditions, she studies and practises them and learns the Maori language. Koro begins to teach some local first-born boys from the village in the
25 'old way', they get lessons in stick-fighting, storytelling and chanting. Koro hopes that one of them will be able to become Whangara's future chief. He refuses to let the unhappy Pai take part in the lessons. —C—

30 When whales become stranded on the beach, Koro is afraid that this means the end of his tribe. The people from the village try to pull the whales back to sea, but their efforts fail. Pai, however, doesn't give up. —D— When she rides on a whale just like the tribe's ancestor Paikea, Koro understands that
35 her courage and gifts can save his people's traditions. 'I should have known she is the one,' he admits.

Whale Rider is a film based on the novel by Maori writer Witi Ihimaera, which came out in 1987.

Niki Caro, who wrote the screenplay and directed
40 the film, is a white New Zealander. —E—

The film is a story about love, rejection and revolt, but also about Maori culture and its survival in a modern society. It shows that change is necessary, but that change need not destroy tradition. The film
45 has been successful at international film festivals and has won several awards. It has been described as the most successful New Zealand film ever. The actress who played Pai, Keisha Castle-Hughes, also experienced great success. She became the youngest
50 actress ever to be nominated for the Best Actress Oscar. She was only 13 years old at the time and it was her first acting role.

SKILLS TRAINING: READING 1

1 Where does it go?

Which of the following sentences (1–5) fit into the gaps (A–E)? Write the correct letter in the box.

1 She prepared for the film by learning about Maori culture and studying te reo, the Maori language, at Auckland University.
2 She talks to the whales and is able to lead them into deep water.
3 Since then the first-born son of his descendants has always been the chief of Whangara, a fishing village on the eastern coast.
4 Knowing Pai's character and courage, Grandmother Flowers continues to understand and encourage her.
5 'Go. Get away from here,' he tells her angrily.

2 Who is it?

Find the right name – Koro, Flowers or Pai – for each sentence.

1 _____ doesn't give up her dream.
2 _____ thinks the idea of a female ruler is against tradition.
3 _____ doesn't agree with her husband.
4 _____ is loved by all her relatives except the one whose love she needs most.
5 _____ is worried about the death of the Maori culture and traditions.
6 _____ has to struggle against strict traditions.

3 What is true?

Read the text and tick (✓) the correct endings to the sentences. Be careful, sometimes more than one ending is correct.

1 Grandfather Koro is disappointed because …
  A ☐ his son goes off to Europe.
  B ☐ he wants a grandson.
  C ☐ the Maori stories seem to be wrong.

2 Koro begins to teach the local boys because …
  A ☐ Pai doesn't like the Maori traditions.
  B ☐ he wants to find Whangara's future chief and train him.
  C ☐ the boys really love the old traditions.

3 When whales get stranded on the beach, …
  A ☐ Koro finishes teaching the boys.
  B ☐ Pai manages to lead them back into deep water.
  C ☐ the villagers try to help them.

4 Niki Caro …
  A ☐ wrote the novel *Whale Rider*.
  B ☐ wrote the screenplay and directed the film.
  C ☐ learned the Maori language.

4 In other words

Find words or expressions from the text which mean the same as the words in brackets.

1 Her father (leaves New Zealand to travel) _____ to Europe.
2 Koro can't accept that Pai might become chief because she is (a girl) _____ .
3 Grandmother Flowers (doesn't agree with him) _____ .
4 When Pai gets older, she (really wants) _____ to earn her grandfather's respect.
5 He (doesn't want to) _____ let Pai take part in the lessons.
6 The people from the village try to pull the whales back to sea, but (they don't succeed although they work hard) _____ .

SKILLS TRAINING: READING 1

5 Find the words

Find the missing words. They are in the text or in exercise 1.

1 tell a lie → tell the truth ● succeed → _____
2 know → knowledge ● reject → _____
3 test → exam ● reach → _____
4 memory → remember ● death → _____
5 death → birth ● ancestor → _____
6 prefer → like better ● rescue → _____
7 protection → protect ● refusal → _____
8 eventually → finally ● some → _____
9 solve → solution ● lead → _____
10 sell → sale ● survive → _____

6 Feelings

1 Find the English translations. The words are in the text or in exercise 1.

1 *entschlossen* _____
2 *warmherzig* _____
3 *verärgert* _____

feelings

4 *enttäuscht* _____
5 *unglücklich* _____
6 *besorgt* _____

2 Explain which characters from the film feel this way and why.

1 _____
2 _____
3 _____
4 _____
5 _____
6 _____

7 Whales in Whangara

Beantworte die folgenden Fragen in ganzen deutschen Sätzen.

1 *Was lernt man über den Stammvater Paikea? (zwei Details)*

_____

2 *Was wird Koro klar, als seine Enkelin die Wale rettet? (zwei Details)*

_____

3 *Wie hat sich die Regisseurin Niki Caro auf den Film ‚Whale Rider' vorbereitet?*

_____

4 *Welche unterschiedlichen Themen werden im Film behandelt? (fünf)*

_____

SKILLS TRAINING: READING 2

Eminem

NACH UNIT 3

Kids all over the world love him, their parents hate him. His lyrics are often angry, nasty and offensive. Eminem raps about violence and crime, sex and drug use, pain, murder and death. Many people have been really upset by his lyrics. —A— His style is black rap, but he is white and he's become the million-selling king of rap from Detroit.

His success story started in 1999 when he brought out *The Slim Shady LP* and won two Grammy awards in 2000. 2000 was also the year in which his next album, *The Marshall Mathers LP*, sold five million copies in the first month in the US alone. His third album, *The Eminem Show*, was also very successful and won the Grammy for the Best Rap Album in 2003. —B—

But is he really a bad boy or is he just trying to shock us? Eminem himself believes he is the new Elvis Presley. Just like Elvis 50 years ago, he has been described as a 'white man singing black music' and a danger to young people. —C— Both of them also created their own sound and sold millions of records.

Eminem's life has always been turbulent. His real name is Marshall Bruce Mathers III. He was born in Kansas City, Missouri, in 1972 and had a tough childhood. —D— 'We kept moving because my mother never had a job,' says Eminem. 'We kept getting kicked out of every house we were in.' Finally he and his mother settled in Detroit. Marshall was a quiet, shy boy. He wasn't a good student and he preferred to read cartoons and listen to rap music. He was often the victim of bullying at school and was attacked by his black classmates. —E— At the age of 13, he went to his first hip-hop concert and then started writing his own lyrics. He soon developed his own style and started recording songs.

At the age of 16, he dropped out of Lincoln High School. He then did various minimum wage jobs while concentrating on rap. He had problems getting on with his mother at that time. His hatred towards her is expressed in several of his songs. Eminem also has a difficult relationship with his ex-wife Kim, who lived with him and his mother from the age of twelve. They got married in 1999, but divorced two years later before marrying and divorcing once again in 2006. Eminem has, however, been a caring father for their daughter, Hailie Jade, born on Christmas Day 1995. He's even written a song about their relationship, *Hailie's Song*. —F—

Most of Eminem's songs are autobiographical. In 2002 he also starred in *8 Mile*, a film about his life and about growing up in Detroit. The film has won several awards, including the Oscar for Best Original Song.

Three years later, it was reported that he was thinking about ending his rapping career, but shortly afterwards Eminem announced that he wasn't planning to retire in the near future. Some fans refused to believe this when his album *Curtain Call: The Hits* came out in 2005. —G— Then in 2007, 50 Cent, another big-time rap star who Eminem has produced songs for, announced, 'Eminem's making new music. I've heard a few songs, and it's hot.'

So, what is the secret behind Eminem's success? Some people think he is the anti-hero that wants to shock those Americans who love their country. Parents often say he is dangerous for their children. They think his records should be banned. However, Eminem is a hero for millions of teenagers who feel out of place and not listened to in adult society. They have had similar life experiences and he makes them feel that they are not alone.

Eminem in the film *8 Mile*

SKILLS TRAINING: READING 2

1 The Eminem story

Which of the following sentences (1–6) fit into the gaps (A–G) in the text? Write the correct letter in the box. Be careful, you don't need all the letters.

1 As he was very small for his age, he could only fight back with words. ☐
2 One of the tracks on it was called *When I'm gone*. ☐
3 They think he stands for hate and intolerance. ☐
4 Both were born poor, and both singers grew to love black music. ☐
5 He has never met his father and was brought up by his mother, Debbie Mathers. ☐
6 Now the critics could no longer deny his talent. ☐

2 True, false or not in the text?

Read the following statements and decide if they are true, false or not in the text. Tick (✓) the correct box.

	True	False	Not in the text
1 Lots of people have been upset by Eminem's lyrics.	☐	☐	☐
2 His album *The Marshall Mathers LP* sold five million copies in the first two months.	☐	☐	☐
3 In some ways Eminem can be compared to Elvis Presley.	☐	☐	☐
4 Eminem's mother didn't think he was very talented.	☐	☐	☐
5 Before Eminem and his mother moved to Detroit, they had lived in the same place since 1972.	☐	☐	☐
6 At school life wasn't always easy for the rapper.	☐	☐	☐
7 Eminem now lives with his daughter.	☐	☐	☐
8 His songs help young people feel less lonely.	☐	☐	☐

3 Complete the sentences

Finish these sentences using information from the text.

1 Lots of people have been upset by Eminem's lyrics because …
   _____
   _____.

2 The young Eminem couldn't settle in one place because …
   _____.

3 You can compare Eminem to Elvis Presley because both …
   _____
   _____.

4 After school Eminem didn't earn much money because …
   _____.

5 When *Curtain Call: The Hits* came out, some fans …
   _____.

6 Millions of teenagers love Eminem because …
   _____.

SKILLS TRAINING: READING 2

4 Find the mistakes

There are four words in the text below that shouldn't be there. If a line is correct, tick (✓) it. If a word shouldn't be there, underline it and write it on the line.

When Eminem started to appear on to shows and on radio stations in Detroit, the rap scene that was completely dominated by blacks. Today most people would agree that Eminem's music has made history. His lyrics have always caused a lot of public discussion, but Eminem says they shouldn't be taken seriously. Some of his critics say that one of the few of positive things is that his songs aren't the racist.

5 Which word is it?

Find the correct word from the text.

1 the words of a song: _____
2 to make somebody worry or feel unhappy is to make someone: _____
3 to go and live in another house or flat: _____
4 being nervous and not saying much when there are strangers: _____
5 a person who is in the same class as you at school: _____
6 a person who is 18 or older: _____

6 His life so far

Finde heraus, was Eminem in den angegebenen Jahren jeweils gemacht hat oder was ihm passiert ist. Schreibe Stichpunkte auf Deutsch.

1972 _____
1985 _____
1988 _____
1995 _____
1999 (zwei Details) _____
_____
2000 (zwei Details) _____
_____
2001 _____
2002 _____
2003 _____
2005 (zwei Details) _____
_____
2006 _____
2007 _____

SKILLS TRAINING: SPEAKING

Work with a partner. Partner A looks at this page. Partner B looks at page 54.

1 The same but different

Partner A
Your photograph shows some pupils in their English lesson. Your partner has the same photograph, but with ten differences. Try to find the differences without looking at their photograph. Ask questions and circle the differences.

2 The office

Partner A
Describe this picture to your partner in detail. Your partner has the same picture, but most objects are missing and have to be drawn on. Explain where the things are without pointing to the picture. Remember to use prepositions of place (in front of, behind, next to, to the left of, on, under …).

SKILLS TRAINING: SPEAKING

Work with a partner. Partner B looks at this page. Partner A looks at page 53.

1   The same but different

Partner B
Your photograph shows some pupils in their English lesson. Your partner has the same photograph, but with ten differences. Try to find the differences without looking at their photograph. Ask questions and circle the differences.

2   The office

Partner B
Listen very carefully to your partner and draw the missing things in the correct place on the picture. Then compare your picture with your partner's.

SKILLS TRAINING: SPEAKING

3   Be careful down under!

1 Your best friend is planning a holiday in Australia. As you've heard about some of the dangers that travellers might meet down under, you can give lots of information. Try to warn him/her. Get into groups and deal with one of the topics below: A – The beach, B – The animals, C – The outback. Practise warning your friend by using the information and pictures given. Your group has to find a total of ten statements about these dangers. Discuss the dangers and take notes.

2 Form new groups of three with a member from each group (A, B, C). Everyone is new here and – just like your friend – needs lots of information on each of the topics. Each member of the new group (member A, member B and member C) makes ten statements about the dangers he/she has learned about. The other two members ask for details. Then decide together which dangers your friend is most likely to meet and how they can protect themselves.

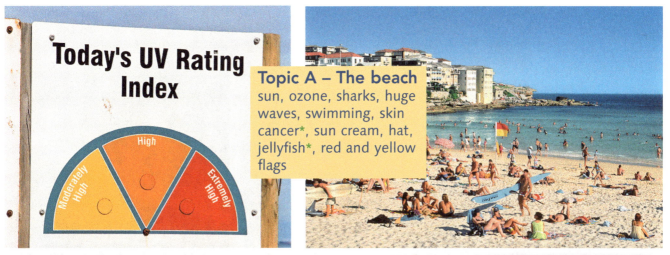

Topic A – The beach
sun, ozone, sharks, huge waves, swimming, skin cancer*, sun cream, hat, jellyfish*, red and yellow flags

Topic B – The animals
spiders, kangaroos, crocodiles, snakes, beetles*, poisonous, check boots and rucksacks, hide in old wood

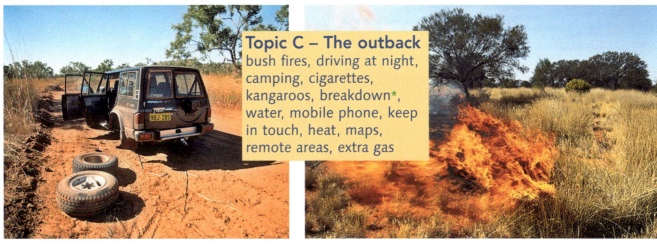

Topic C – The outback
bush fires, driving at night, camping, cigarettes, kangaroos, breakdown*, water, mobile phone, keep in touch, heat, maps, remote areas, extra gas

*NEW: cancer – *Krebs*; jellyfish – *Qualle*; beetle – *Käfer*; breakdown – *Panne*

SKILLS TRAINING: SPEAKING

4 Holidays in Canada

Vancouver is the largest city in the province of British Columbia (BC) and the third largest city in Canada. It's surrounded by water on three sides, and in the east there is the Coast Mountain Range. You can enjoy spectacular natural scenery and one of the mildest climates in Canada.

You and a friend are going to spend a two-week summer holiday in Vancouver. Even though there is so much to see and do in the city, you want to see the surroundings, too. You have found the Vancouver Sightseeing and City Tours website where they offer different day or half-day trips. Discuss two of the tours with your friend and decide which tour you want to go on.

TOUR 1: GROUSE MOUNTAIN, NORTH SHORE & CAPILANO SUSPENSION BRIDGE

DAILY TOURS FEB 28 – NOV 14 2:00 PM 5-HOUR TOUR: ADULT $79.00 CHILD $46.00

Take the **Grouse Mountain Skyride**. Rise to a viewpoint 1,200 metres above the city and enjoy the breathtaking panoramic view.

Cross **Vancouver Harbour** on the SeaBus, and see Canada's 'Gateway to the Pacific'. Enjoy the view of the city's skyline and mountains.

Visit **Capilano Suspension Bridge**, Vancouver's man-made wonder built in 1888. Stand on the walkway 230 feet above the canyon floor of the Capilano River.

TOUR 2: WHISTLER MOUNTAINS & FORESTS

DAILY TOURS MAY 1 – OCT 11 8:00 AM 10 HOUR TOUR: ADULT $99.00 CHILD $66.00

Bus ride to **Whistler** via the spectacular Sea-to-Sky Highway. Stops including Shannon Falls, the third highest waterfall in BC.

Sightseeing Tour of **Whistler Village**, the premier ski resort in North America. See where the 2010 Olympic Games will take place. Free time to visit the village shops.

Walk through the amazing **Old Rain Forest** where a guide will explain the magic of the forest to you. Enjoy the mountain scenery.